REBUILDING AMERICA'S WORKFORCE

Business Strategies to Close the
Competitive Gap

REBUILDING AMERICA'S WORKFORCE

Business Strategies to Close the Competitive Gap

William H. Kolberg
President and Chief Executive Officer
The National Alliance of Business
Foster C. Smith
Senior Vice President
The National Alliance of Business

BUSINESS ONE IRWIN
Homewood, Illinois 60430

Sponsoring editor: Cynthia A. Zigmund
Project editor: Karen J. Nelson
Production manager: Mary Jo Parke
Jacket designer: Tim Kaage
Compositor: Precision Typographers
Typeface: 11/14 Palatino
Printer: Arcata Graphics/Kingsport

Library of Congress Cataloging-in-Publication Data

Kolberg, William H.
    Rebuilding America's workforce : business strategies to close the competitive gap / William H. Kolberg, Foster C. Smith.
        p.   cm.
    Includes bibliographical references.
    ISBN 1-55623-622-0
    1. Manpower planning—United States. 2. United States—Economic policy—1981- 3. Human capital—United States. 4. Industry and state—United States. 5. Occupational training—United States.
    6. Competition, International. I. Smith, Foster C. II. Title
    HF5549.5.M3K65   1992
    331.1'0973—dc20   91-27859

Printed in the United States of America
1 2 3 4 5 6 7 8 9 0 K 8 7 6 5 4 3 2 1

FOREWORD

The end of one century and the beginning of another is a natural time for reflection and anticipation. As we approach the year 2000, much is being written about where we have been as a nation—and where we are going. This watershed period stimulates experts to interpret historical and current events in order to extrapolate the future.

There is, of course, much activity from which to extrapolate. Consider:

startling breakthroughs in communications and computer technology and in many scientific disciplines;

expanding frontiers in space;

sudden and dramatic political changes in Eastern Europe and the Middle East, and

the flourishing of the global marketplace.

Young people today are growing up in a dramatically different world. Not all aspects of our lives have improved, however.

In several critical areas, America is failing to stay abreast of the times. American students are not as well-educated as many of their foreign counterparts. American workers are not as skilled as those in a growing number of foreign countries. American businesses are not always as efficient as those in other countries with whom they compete. Too many of our educational and business strategies and methodologies differ little from those of a half century ago. Unless corrected, these deficiencies will continue to undermine America's economic foundation.

We are all familiar with the competitive disadvantages we

increasingly face—disadvantages that accrue to a large degree from the higher commitment to effective education and business practices found elsewhere in the world. The fact is that if we are to be globally competitive in the future, we cannot perpetuate the usages of the past.

Business is not the only beneficiary of an educational system that effectively prepares young people for tomorrow's world, but it is clearly a primary beneficiary. Certainly our business and economic system cannot survive over the long term if our educational system does not properly prepare tomorrow's leaders. We can no longer rely on old approaches to prepare people for work, and to provide products and services. Change must occur. We cannot expect young people to prepare themselves for the future's work when all we provide is an education system built on the past. Business leaders must make the investments necessary to upgrade the skills of workers, and then adopt business strategies that take full advantage of those skills.

The views I express are not singularly mine. I was privileged to serve on President Reagan's Commission on Industrial Competitiveness. The Commission concluded that not only was America losing its competitive advantages, but that it also was losing the worldwide race to develop skilled workers and business leaders.

In the past decade, we have seen profound and fundamental changes in the way American business is managed. Even many of the largest of our businesses have abandoned their highly centralized, top-heavy organizations in favor of smaller units managed in an entrepreneurial fashion. Employees at all levels have been empowered beyond the wildest dreams of their predecessors of 25 or 50 years ago.

Such changes, however, do not come easily. They require discipline, a long-term strategic outlook, and additional investment in plants, equipment and research, and development. Changes also require patience.

I wish I could attribute the changes we have made entirely to a new generation of leaders enlightened in contemporary business management by a contemporary educational system. Unfortunately, I cannot. These changes often were made under crisis conditions by over-leveraged companies that were forced to become more efficient in order to survive. Others, learning from hard-won experience, saw the future clearly and chose to prepare for it in a more orderly fashion.

For whatever reason, American business is in transition. It is becoming leaner. It is reorganizing to become more efficient. It is retraining its workers and empowering them. It is investing in the future by investing in the people who will lead in the years ahead. The question yet to be answered, however, is whether American business can make these changes fast enough to remain competitive in a global economy.

I believe that the highest priority for those of us in American business in the decades ahead is to train and motivate our employees in order to ensure the future primacy of our nation in the world community. If we fail, we confront the likelihood that our political and economic systems will decline.

Rebuilding America's Workforce is a powerful advocate for the role business must play in transforming America's workforce into one that will serve us well in the 21st century. It correctly argues that today's business leaders have a stewardship obligation to America's future. It is an obligation that must be met principally by working to place our educational and business systems on a globally competitive and responsive foundation.

John D. Ong
Chairman and Chief Executive Officer
The BFGoodrich Company

ACKNOWLEDGMENTS

The authors wish to acknowledge and thank a number of colleagues at the National Alliance of Business for their assistance and useful critiques during preparation of this book.

Terri Bergman, Tom Lindsley, and Gary Moore contributed substantial research and text in the areas of education, labor policy, and school-to-work activity. The senior staff of the Alliance provided constructive editorial and policy comments. Finally, Margaret George was invaluable throughout the process in researching sources and statistics and in helping us organize the manuscript.

At Business One/Irwin, Cynthia Zigmund and Jean Geracie demonstrated unusual patience and insight as they shepherded the authors through the publication process.

William H. Kolberg
Foster C. Smith

CONTENTS

INTRODUCTION

This book addresses the problems American business now confronts because a lack of national human-investment policies and practices during the past 25 years has created a noncompetitive public school system, a noncompetitive worker-training system, and noncompetitive workplace organizations. This neglect has allowed our economic competitors in other countries to draw abreast of the United States in productivity. If action is not taken soon, the United States will slip from first place to an also-ran competitive economy by the end of the decade.

The essential difference that has developed between these nations and the Untied States during the past several decades is that the national consensus of our foreign competitors has been to develop fully the intelligence and talents of their people. However, the United States has chosen to drift along without consensus, presuming that we can continue economic dominance by sticking with the business and social approaches that propelled us into first place earlier in the century. For the most part, we have been satisfied with the status quo.

This decline in clearcut economic superiority has already had a profound effect on our markets and on our standard of living. Unless we implement a new set of national public and private human-investment policies, we will continue to lose ground.

This is not the first book to sound the competitiveness claxon, and hopefully it will not be the last, because our ability to reverse the trends of the past quarter century will determine whether we will be able to maintain a reasonable standard of living in this country and maintain political stability in the decades ahead.

There are hopeful signs, however, that America's economic engine has at least shifted into first gear after a decade or two in idle. Manufacturing productivity in the United States grew at a rate of 3.6 percent in the 1980s, which is three times as fast as in the 1970s and comparable to industralized competitor nations.[1] Some leading companies are establishing models for worker retraining and workplace reorganization, which have resulted in improved efficiency and product quality. Federal, state, and local governments are beginning to address problems associated with education and worker training.

The United States must work its way through all the gears, and business must lead the way. This has been the American century and there remains the possibility that the nation can maintain the American dream for another 100 years, but it will take hard work and ingenuity to do so.

The changes needed to maintain U.S. economic leadership will also produce full employment and better-paying jobs. A resurgence in national wealth will lead to environmental improvement, more help for disadvantaged nations, and less international conflict. The ability of the United States to continue its economic leadership will also allow it to continue demonstrating the values of democratic capitalism.

At this moment in time, America's glass is truly half full—during the next 10 years, it will be drained or it will be filled. The business community will determine which future the nation experiences, for it has the leadership needed to ensure progress.

Business must help the nation develop:

- a reorganized workplace, with empowered workers and fewer supervisors
- a lifelong training system for workers
- a world-class education system that produces new workers ready to handle high paying skilled work
- a public-private partnership in every American community, to ensure that the best employees and the best business practices are available.

This syllogism—work organization, trained workers, educated workers—must be established as America's new business paradigm in partnership with federal, state, and local governments.

The need for this critical set of changes has only developed during the past few decades. For most of this century, the United States has led the world in economic growth and has produced an unmatched standard of living. U.S. dominance of world commerce reached a crescendo after World War II and, in fact, in 1958 J. J. Servan-Schreiber warned his fellow French about the economic invasion of Europe by Americans: "American industry has gauged the terrain and is now rolling from Naples to Amsterdam with the ease and speed of Israeli tanks in the Sinai desert."[2]

The increases in U.S. output and productivity during the 20th century were fueled by high rates of savings and capital investment, low inflation and low interest rates, rapid technological advances, and, perhaps most importantly, the skills and muscle power of a burgeoning population.

The nation could not have become an economic powerhouse without a diverse, educated and mobile work force—the product of generations of immigrants who worked hard and expected to see their children lead better lives.

But, something has gone awry. Baseball fans used to cry "break up the Yankees" because the teams of the 1920s and 1930s seemed to be invincible. Well, no longer is anyone demanding to break up the Yankees—neither the baseball team nor the Yankee business team. U.S. competitiveness is declining and we will lose our economic leadership within this decade if business does not take action soon. Evidence of this includes the following:

1. Wage rates in the United States are lower than in Germany, Sweden, and Denmark and are falling.[3]
2. U.S. productivity growth has ranked last for over a decade compared to other industrialized nations.[4]
3. U.S. school children score in the last quartile in math and science compared to students in all other industrialized nations.[5]

4. The United States is now the world's largest debtor nation with the lowest savings rate among industrialized nations.[6]

These and a multitude of other statistics indicate that U.S. dominance of world commerce peaked some 20 to 30 years ago and that the nation continues on a slippery slide to second-rate status. Moreover, U.S. businesses are in danger of losing dominance in their home market, which remains the largest and richest market in the world.

For several decades, U.S. productivity has risen more slowly than in most other industrialized nations. While the United States still leads the world in productivity in absolute terms, other countries are gaining rapidly. From the period 1950 through 1989, U.S. productivity growth averaged only 1.9 percent per year, which was lower than 13 other competitor countries.[7] At current rates of growth, we will become less productive than a number of these countries during this decade.

Moreover, many of our foreign competitors have shared these productivity gains with their workers. Average wage rates are rising throughout the industrialized community, but they have declined in the United States since 1970. Employers in other countries are achieving efficiencies that allow them to share their higher profits with their skilled employees. In fact, the efficiency gains are so high that countries like Germany and Japan have been able to maintain their competitive edge during the rise of newly industrialized, low-wage countries such as South Korea, Taiwan, and Singapore.

Other nations have continued to upgrade their education standards and expectations for all their youth. They have intensely trained these educated youth and have given them responsibilities congruent with their knowledge and skill.

The basic building block for career preparation is a good education. The U.S. education system has not kept up and is not producing enough high school graduates who are as knowledgeable as their foreign counterparts.

Despite the fact that only 25 percent of our youth graduate from four-year colleges, the United States has consistently placed highest value on white-collar work and has devalued blue-collar work.[8] This value system led our schools to orient their missions to favor college-bound students, and the 75 percent of our youth that never completed college were abandoned.[9]

Complicating efforts to improve the education system is the attitude of many parents. Surveys indicate that three fourths of Americans believe there is something awry with the U.S. school system, but the same percentage believe their local schools are doing a good job.[10]

Despite this lack of grassroots demand, a monumental effort to upgrade U.S. education is underway by those people who comprehend the universality of the education problem and understand the linkages between the quality of U.S. education and the ability of the nation to compete with other nations economically.

These linkages are recognized in other countries. As nations rebuilt their economies after World War II, they emphasized primary and secondary education excellence and established public-private apprenticeship programs to prepare their youth for work. In addition to developing worker skills, they also adopted new forms of work organization, abandoning the system developed in the United States during the early part of this century. They built manufacturing and service businesses that depend on highly trained employees who participate in decision making.

For the most part, U.S. manufacturing businesses have clung to the traditional system of assembly-line processes, not requiring employees to have advanced education and training, but requiring a greater number of employees to produce the same amount of goods as better-trained workers. Too many U.S. companies in service industries have not converted to a customer-oriented culture that allows employees the autonomy to make customer-pleasing decisions that produce higher sales per worker.

Many employers complain that our schools are not preparing students well enough to employ them in these new forms of work organization. Accordingly, many companies have adopted a different approach to hiring. The Commission on the Skills of the American Workforce reports that many U.S. business people don't perceive a serious problem with the quality of workers they hire.[11] These employers claim they are more interested in attitude than they are in aptitude; they want dependable, cheerful workers because they can organize work in a simplistic way to accommodate the intelligence and skills of the workers. As the report of the Commission put it, U.S. businesses have adopted a "low skills, low wages" outlook.[12]

The decline of U.S. competitiveness due to this outlook has been obscured by an eight-year-long economic expansion fueled by borrowing and an expanding work force that consumed more goods and services. With the unprecedented growth of two-income families in the United States, the principal financial effect of this decline was masked. The fact is, adjusted for inflation, average weekly wages of workers in the United States have fallen 12 percent during the past 20 years, reflecting the need for U.S. companies to lower their costs in order to be competitive.[13]

To offset a decline in real pay, more family members must work. More than half of all married women have jobs now, up from one third in 1960.[14] Fifty-five percent of our teenagers now work, up from 48 percent in 1968.[15] During this same period, many Americans didn't keep up—the number of families with incomes below the poverty level rose 24 percent between 1973 and 1986.[16] Because family incomes in the United States on average have kept slightly ahead of inflation, there has been little agitation for change. So far, there is not enough recognition of the problem. On an international basis, the U.S. standard of living has grown only 33 percent since 1972, the slowest growth rate of the seven countries comprising the Group of Seven industrialized countries. Japan's grew nearly 80 percent during the same period, Italy by 64 percent and Germany by 48 percent.[17] The United States maintains the highest standard of living of these seven countries, but the gap is narrowing. In 1989, the other nations averaged a standard of living 74 percent of the United States, up from 64 percent in 1972.[18]

As the true place of U.S. business in world commerce is recognized and as the standard of living deteriorates for many

Americans, more and more people are asking how this could have happened: How could a nation that emerged from a world war in a hugely dominant position fritter away its opportunities to the point where we are now dependent on a weak dollar to generate export sales and dependent on lower and lower wage rates to compete with more efficient foreign businesses? How did we slide into what MIT economist Paul R. Krugman calls an "age of diminished expectations"?[19]

The answer to these questions is complex. It was a long process, partially the result of the optimistic U.S. nature, partially the result of perceived invincible economic dominance, and partially the result of the intelligence of our industrial competitors.

It is impossible to pinpoint a moment of sea change in a nation as large and as diverse as the United States, but two trends of the 1960s indicate how U.S. business began slipping. First, U.S. business failed to recognize what many have called the third industrial revolution and did not reorganize the workplace to gain the efficiencies garnered by our foreign competitors. Secondly, the systems for preparing the nation's youth for work did not stay competitive with the public/private partnerships developed in competitor nations.

U.S. education and training progress stalled, resulting in a workforce not skilled enough to handle new work systems and new technologies. The confluence of these two oversights has resulted in a steady erosion of U.S. productivity, workforce competence, and the standard of living in this country.

It isn't too surprising that U.S. business didn't alter its practices radically in the post-war period. Because of the nation's economic dominance after World War II, there appeared to be little need to reorganize the workplace to take advantage of new technology and new work practices. Consequently, there was no demand for the U.S. education system to continue its historic rate of progress in delivering more learning to additional students; it has been stalled since the 1960s. For the same reason, U.S. businesses did not undertake new training for frontline workers and develop partnerships with schools to link students with work.

Now, there is a work organization gap, a training gap, a

public-policy gap, and an education gap between the United States and other countries. The problem is serious because workers are now imbedded in the workforce who require remedial education before they can be trained to operate in these new work environments. It will take years to develop a better education system in this country and a new school-to-work system that presents business with new workers who are as capable as their international counterparts.

The need for a fundamental change in so many parts of the U.S. social fabric is heightened by development of still another worldwide business trend. It is now economically feasible to design and manufacture products in many countries throughout the world and then to sell them in nearly all international markets. Ownership of natural resources is not a prerequisite for comparative advantage; technology is available nearly everywhere and can be faxed anywhere; capital pools are available on an international scale; low-cost, literate labor is readily available. Now, a New Global Commerce System is in place that is homogenizing business activity without regard to political borders. And the ease of operating in this New Global Commerce system grows each year.

What this means is that companies around the world are deciding every day where products will be designed, engineered, assembled, and sold. In turn, this means that many U.S. workers now compete for their jobs on a worldwide scale—they will either compete for these jobs on the basis of low wages or on the basis of high skills. To maintain America's standard of living—to get the productivity growth engine into high gear—the nation must undertake a massive effort to upgrade worker skills and the added value component of their input. At the moment, most U.S. workers cannot compete on the basis of low wages or high skills. Our low-wage workforce is paid more than workers in many other countries, and our average workers are not educated or trained as well as their foreign counterparts.

The business community must galvanize itself and all of the United States into action programs that stem the rising tide of mediocrity engulfing the nation. Business must become an advocate for public-policy changes and reorder the way it approaches work and workers. If U.S. business does not meet this challenge, the competitive gap it already confronts will widen, and the nation will become a second-tier country with a declining standard of living.

To date, businesses have reacted differently to the changes occurring in international commerce. Some companies recognize the danger signs and have taken action to repair their competitive postures. Others, particularly smaller businesses, recognize the dangers but don't have the resources needed to take action; and still others refuse to admit they have a problem.

A number of U.S. companies have seen the handwriting on the wall. Whether they were confronted with more efficient foreign competition or simply comprehended the wisdom of improving efficiency, they have demonstrated that U.S. workers can be trained to compete with workers anywhere in the world. They have developed a new paradigm for work organization and worker involvement.

Leading edge companies in the United States, such as Motorola, General Electric, and IBM, realize that to compete in the global marketplace they must reorder their priorities to emphasize quality products, customer service, and better efficiency. They quickly discovered that they could not achieve these goals without a dedicated, skilled workforce that was unemcumbered by bureaucracies.

This meant decentralizing authority and making investments in improving the skills of newly empowered employees, both blue-collar employees in factories and "gray" collar employees in service industries. In short, they began forming what the Commission on the Skills of the American Workforce calls "high-performance work organizations."[20] The Commission estimates that only about 5 percent of U.S. companies had formed these new organizations by 1990.[21]

The value of intensive training and decentralization of decision making was vividly demonstrated during the recent Gulf War. U.S. youth proved that they could be trained to operate the most sophisticated machinery on earth. In many engagements, U.S. troops outperformed their enemy counterparts who were equipped with equipment that was as good or better than ours;

the battleground difference was the skill of our people.

The ability of employers to take advantage of the native intelligence and energy of their workers as effectively as the military establishment will not be realized unless U.S. businesses revolutionize their methods of organizing work, a system that has not changed in over 70 years in this country, but has changed markedly in most other industrialized nations.

The present system of work organization in most U.S. businesses was developed in the early part of the 20th century, with emphasis on time and motion studies and the assembly line. The system segmented work activity into a series of simple tasks that matched the ability of workers of that period—a fourth-grade education and no skills training. Better-educated employees planned the work and handled other "thinking" jobs such as machine design, purchasing, quality control, and administration. It was a brilliant system for wringing the optimum amount of work from wage earners.

Since World War II, however, there has been a revolution in work organization in other countries. In concert with development of new technology that depended on better-educated and highly trained workers, our industrialized competitors reorganized work systems in factories and offices to take advantage of the intelligence and skills of their frontline workers, lowering the need for administrative employees. The result has been better productivity and higher-quality products.[22] They were able to achieve these efficiencies through a close relationship between business and government. Most of our foreign competitor nations established human resource policies which link school to work and which encourage continuous worker training. For the most part, the only national training systems in the United States are established for disadvantaged and displaced workers.

This disparate development between the United States and other industrialized nations can be explained many ways. Some of these nations have more socialistic cultural traditions, which led them to central planning and control. Others, lacking natural resources, have had to depend on the ingenuity of their people to gain an economic advantage. Regardless of the reason for the disparity, the common denominator is a greater dependence on

FIGURE I–1

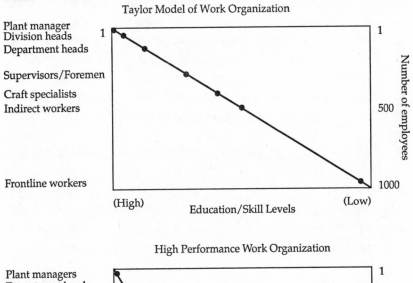

Taylor Model of Work Organization

Plant manager
Division heads
Department heads

Supervisors/Foremen

Craft specialists
Indirect workers

Frontline workers

(High)   Education/Skill Levels   (Low)

Number of employees
1 — 500 — 1000

High Performance Work Organization

Plant managers
Department heads

Team leaders

Frontline workers

(High)   Education/Skill Levels   (Low)

Number of employees
1 — 1000

This is an idealized schematic representation of the advantages of a high-performance work organization staffed by well-trained workers. As education and skills increase, staff size drops without a loss of output. Staff size drops because (1) fewer supervisory and support personnel are required, and (2) fewer frontline workers are required. In a decentralized high-performance work environment, frontline workers operate with less oversight and are empowered to implement a broader range of activities. Additional measures, such as just-in-time delivery and total quality, also reduce expenses associated with work-in-process, scrap, and rework.

workers and a concomitant higher order of education, school-to-work transition, and work systems that exploit worker knowledge.

The importance of reorganizing work and upgrading employee skills in the United States cannot be overemphasized. Of those Americans who will be at work in the year 2000, 85 percent are already on the job.[23] Consequently, reeducation, training, and work reorganization must occur even as the nation restructures its education system and establishes a school-to-work system. This will be an enormous financial burden on companies at a time when they are faced with tough, efficient foreign competition.

Accordingly, as part of a new national consensus that recognizes the importance of investments in our human capital, tax credits should be made available for training of frontline workers.

Reorganizing the workplace and retraining frontline workers are critically important in the short run, and improving the systems that provide new workers is critical for the future. Systems must be constructed to provide school-to-work skill training for noncollege-bound students, and the U.S. education system must be upgraded to stay abreast of the needs of the workforce.

Traditionally, U.S. youth that did not attend college were guided into work by family influence and local work prospects. Sons of mill workers and auto workers followed their fathers into the factories. Some learned skills through labor union apprenticeship programs, and others were taught right on the factory floor. Most did not require guidance or specialized training because most work was organized in a manner to accommodate the average 16- or 18-year-old person with less than 12 years of education.

During the past several decades, government programs have been established to train the disadvantaged and other unemployed people who need help in returning to the workforce, but the United States has never developed a comprehensive method of developing the skills of youth to match the needs of the workplace. In other countries, where national consensus allows a more regimented approach to work preparation, there are sophisticated systems in place that combine private-sector and public-sector input to the development of skilled workers.

Although the cultural differences between the United States and these competitor nations would not allow us to clone these systems, undoubtedly we must develop mechanisms of some sort to provide better preparation for prospective workers.

As things now stand, a typical noncollege-bound teenager leaves high school with some knowledge and no skills. He or she drifts in and out of various educational experiences and jobs for a number of years until at some point a decision is made to learn a craft or particular skill that pays enough to support a family. The average age of students at the nation's community colleges is 29, evidence that we are losing nearly 10 years of productive contribution by those that seek improvement to their lives.[24] The cost of lost productivity, lost payroll taxes, and lost social dignity cannot be computed.

The United States must devise a school-to-work transition system that combines our schools, business, and government in a manner to provide help to those who wish to lead productive, rewarding lives without a college degree. Wages will not rise until we educate and enhance the skills of these frontline workers.

To achieve this coordination, a comprehensive community human resource development system must be established in every community in the United States. All sectors of the community must join in a partnership to ensure that the nation's youth are properly prepared for work, to help businesses retrain their workers throughout their careers, and to assist small businesses with modern management techniques. New tax money would not be needed for this system; current programs operated by federal, state, and local governments could be organized and focused on the needs of each community in a manner to upgrade the efficiency of local businesses.

Although the framework for this new approach to local economic development would be national in scope and result from a national consensus that U.S. business competitiveness must be improved, implementation would be decentralized to serve the characteristics of each locale.

If the problems of workplace reform, education reform, and training reform are not resolved, the social costs of this situation will be intolerable to Americans. Low-skilled, poorly educated workers stuck in mindless jobs will join forces with those who are jobless to demand radical change. We will discover the truth of the belief that uneducated people cannot participate effectively in a democracy. The growing disparity in wealth between the upper one third of Americans and the remainder will not be tolerated indefinitely; 30 percent of Americans now earn nearly 60 percent of the national income.[25]

To reverse these ominous trends, to close the widening competitive gap, a paradigm shift must occur during this decade. New models of education and efficient worker training must be developed. A nationwide business/government system must be established to focus on occupational-skills development.

This shift will not occur until business begins to make new demands: business must demand that our schools produce first-class students who go to work ready to learn skills and crafts; business must demand that the nation develop a skills-training system that marries the public and private sectors.

The final competitive edge in international commerce is the quality of a nation's workforce. If U.S. businesses do not reorganize the workplace during the decade of the 1990s and train the workforce, the United States will inevitably slip into a low-skill, low-wage category of nations. Lower standards of living will follow. It would be ironic if, in the years ahead, U.S. companies were forced to move high-skill, highly paid jobs to other countries because they could not find enough qualified workers in the United States.

U.S. business must lead the effort to generate awareness of this dilemma. It must lead in building a new societal concern for human investment even as it remolds its work patterns and its thinking about the role of people in the workplace. American cultural values must change and we must embrace the concept of lifelong learning and value learning in school and on the job. Without this change, the United States will not close the competitive gap.

PART 1

THE COMPETITIVE GAP

CHAPTER 1

OVERVIEW

U.S. business is at an historic crossroads. During the coming decade, the fate of thousands of companies and millions of employees will be determined as business people decide how to compete in the New Global Commerce System. There is an entirely new paradigm for business based on global markets and invisible national borders. Those businesses that understand the paradigm and exploit it will succeed, and the others will fail.

The New Global Commerce System is one in which possession of natural resources, capital, technology, and information are less important to achieving success in international trade. These former prerequisites for business success are either less important or now readily available to businesses throughout the world. The old barriers have fallen. Consider these examples:

- Mitsubishi automobiles that were designed in Japan are assembled in Thailand and now being sold in the United States under the Plymouth trademark.
- GE microwave ovens are sold in the United States after being designed and assembled in South Korea by Samsung.
- Kodak-brand videotapes made by Matsushita are marketed worldwide.
- In a reverse twist, Japan-based Minolta is selling an instant camera manufactured by Polaroid.

Robert B. Reich, in his book *The Work of Nations*, describes what he has labeled the Global Web in which businesses now operate. The Global Web allows them to choose where they will design, engineer, fabricate, and assemble products for sale in any country. And the web is not limited to manufactured goods—to a growing degree, service-based companies are moving labor-intensive activity to areas of the world where the ratio of labor costs and labor ability meet most effectively.[1]

This sea change in business operations has been made possible by satellites, low-cost shipping, worldwide availability of capital, worldwide technology development, and low-cost, capable labor pools. Although only the largest corporations are taking advantage of this flexibility, smaller companies are beginning to, especially in the electronics industries.

The prime example of this phenomenon is the PC industry, where small companies can enter the market practically overnight and succeed spectacularly. Compaq computer is the best known of the companies that accomplished this—it entered the market in 1983 and by 1990 it had revenues of $3 billion.[2] Compaq, like most companies in the PC industry, does very little manufacturing.[3] It purchases most of its components and has final units assembled overseas; it sells through a dealer network.[4]

As development, design, transportation, and other costs continue to decline around the world, smaller and smaller businesses will be able to take advantage of the tumbling barriers. As U.S. businesses make these decisions, the United States confronts hard choices regarding its workforce. With every passing year, more U.S. workers will compete for their jobs in a worldwide pool of workers. To the extent that goods and services can be financed, designed, fabricated, and assembled anywhere, U.S. worker productivity will be a deciding factor on where businesses choose to do their work.

How will business decide to employ the American workforce? Can the American workforce compete with the Singapore workforce? Should it? Can the American workforce complete with the German workforce? Should it?

For the time being, these and other questions are moot. Business has little choice regarding its American workers because the United States does not have a workforce policy—there is no consensus in the United States about the role of workers in our society. Until there is, U.S. business has a Hobson's choice—either spend large amounts of capital providing remedial basic education and training for workers, or try to compete on the basis of low wages with foreign businesses that have better-educated and better-trained workforces.

This situation places U.S. business at a strategic disadvantage when competing with foreign companies. The resulting competitive gap between U.S. and foreign businesses is widening. The history of economic progress in nation after nation has waxed and waned in concert with the productivity of their workers—at a minimum, the ability of a workforce to utilize new technology has governed the pace at which new technology moves into the workplace.

All over the globe, businesses are taking advantage of better-trained workers by empowering them with greater responsibilities that, in turn, are producing greater efficiencies. In the United States, productivity growth has been slowing for two decades. If this gap is not closed, the United States will become a low-wage nation during the next 50 years.

The strategies for reversing this situation and returning the United States to its leadership role are business strategies. Only the business community can articulate the need for better-educated and better-trained employees; only business can establish the public-policy changes that are needed so desperately; only business can change the way it organizes the workplace.

In 1776, Adam Smith in *An Inquiry into the Nature and Causes of the Wealth of Nations* first proposed the notion of national productivity as the determinant of national wealth. He reasoned that nations should export those goods they could produce at a lower cost than others (absolute advantage) and suggested that this labor-productivity advantage could be determined by the percentage of population at work and the "skill, dexterity, and judgment by which labor is generally applied."[5] Two hundred years later, his productivity formula still applies.

Eli Heckscher and Bertil Ohlin built on the work of Smith and David Ricardo to argue the case for *comparative* advantage. Comparative advantage argues that all nations have access to the same technology but have other factors that determine their economic success. Natural resources, capital, land, and the quality of the labor force are among these factors. The idea of comparative advantage is to exploit one's advantages and exchange goods with those that have different advantages.

The idea that each nation should exploit what it had and trade for what it lacked made sense at the time. It was congruent with a great deal of what already existed in the world.

For some 300 years prior to Smith's publication and the subsequent development of this paradigm, the mercantilist system held that a nation must produce all that it consumed to keep money from leaving the country. This philosophy, which fueled the expansionist policies of Spain, France, England, and Holland, led to the establishment of colonies. The idea was that the colonies would ship their natural resources back to the motherland, where they would be converted into products (for sale to the colonists, in many cases). In fact, if England had allowed the American colonies to develop their own economy, including local manufacturing, the Revolution might have occurred much later.

An attractive aspect of this new view of national economics is that it allowed commerce to flow without being a zero-sum game. That is, by capitalizing on their inherent strengths, nations could enter into worldwide trade rather than depend upon building self-sufficient empires. This not only appealed to 18th century business people who suddenly saw immensely larger markets merely by looking at the globe, but also to monarchs who suddenly had less pressure to fund the large armies and navies required to conquer and defend an empire.

For 200 years, nations have striven to fulfill the destiny spelled out for them by the theory of comparative advantage. The theory has been so powerful that some governments continue to form national economic policies based on it. Wars have been conducted to acquire natural resources. Some countries without resources, such as Holland, became traders and then used their wealth and might to acquire colonies with the resources they lacked—a sort of colonialist backwards integration.

There have been wars since—and some in the cause of economic expansion—but as we near the 21st century, the new paradigm obviates war as an economic instrument. Japan, with few natural resources, has achieved the "Greater East Asia Coprosperity Sphere" it sought when it started World War II. And it has done so without firing a shot. It has learned to exploit knowledge and other techniques to build a mighty export machine.

Throughout the modern international trading era, however, greater attention has been applied in most industrialized countries to national productivity, especially as it is affected by workforce productivity.

An important reason for this focus is the changing nature of comparative advantages. Although technology may once have been the only commercial factor available on a global basis, business now operates in an environment where there are very few international barriers to commercial enterprise. As capital, natural resources, distribution, and other elements of business development are acquired more easily on a global basis, companies will expand their markets for products originally intended for consumption in home markets.

Essentially, comparative advantage is being replaced as the principal theory governing international commerce. The new paradigm is under development in Japan and in Western Europe but not in the United States.

At the same time, however, to produce an automobile in Europe or Japan and sell it in the United States at a competitive price means that the producers need some sort of an edge. German and Japanese autos are known for their quality, and there is a market for that feature. But these same producers can also compete on the basis of price, which means they have figured out how to lower costs. Their edge is a workforce educated and trained well enough to produce low-cost cars using less manhours or high-cost cars of superior performance.

Combined with techniques such as just-in-time inventory systems and nearly zero scrap rates, these producers are able to pay their workers as much as U.S. workers and manufacture very expensive cars or cars at lower unit costs.

What has been recognized more rapidly in other nations than in the United States is that a new sort of resource has developed. Knowledge has grown in importance; the ability of a nation's workers, managers, and scientists to add value has become the foundation of the new business paradigm. Moreover, management knowledge of how to organize work and to train workers has itself become a comparative advantage.

Japanese auto plants in the United States are more productive than U.S. auto plants. This ability to reproduce efficiency in other countries provides Japanese management with an extra strategic option—if for some reason it makes more sense to establish manufacturing facilities in another country rather than depend on exports from Japan, Japanese managers know how to do so in a cost-competitive manner.

Sony, with 70 percent of its sales derived from outside Japan, has globally decentralized.[6] Each of its main markets has its own manufacturing facilities.[7] It has 500 foreign subsidiaries and 475 of them are managed by non-Japanese who are operating under Japanese work systems.[8]

Japanese investment strategies are worker-oriented in many ways. Of interest, total Japanese direct investments in European Community nations are about 50 percent wholly owned, newly established companies, but in England 70 percent are wholly owned new companies. Apparently, existing English firms have less to offer, and it makes more sense to the Japanese to train English workers in fresh facilities rather than convert existing work systems and workers.[9]

Until recently, the United States had a history of educating and training its workers in concert with the needs of the workplace to increase productivity. Particularly in the northeast portion of the nation, where free and mandatory education was first legislated, the United States was an early, effective competitor and in the last century exported Yankee ingenuity around the world. Combining technological development with the ability to implement it in factories catapulted the United States to the forefront of the second industrial revolution. By the early part of the 20th century, the country's economic engine was running on all four cylinders—on the way to eight cylinders.

U.S. management methods were unmatched. Working with Henry Ford in his new factories, Frederick W. Taylor was fine-tuning time-and-motion studies that exquisitely matched the ability of U.S. workers to execute their assembly-line assignments. The combination of new machinery, assembly-line science, and mass production enabled Ford to pay the highest wages in the land—the unheard of $5 per day—and sell the lowest-priced automobile.

Through most of this century, the United States has maintained this knowledge-technology-production superiority. Two devastating wars in Europe slowed development there, not because science and knowledge lagged, but because the infrastructures of these lands were twice destroyed. In Eastern Europe, the debilitating drag of communistic central planning offset most of the accomplishment of talented people. In Japan, Samurai cultural history suppressed the latent talents of most people until after World War II, when business Shoguns realized that they had to develop peaceful approaches to economic expansion.

The easy superiority enjoyed by the United States partially flowed from the advantages the country had after World War II. Unlike most industrialized competitor nations, U.S. industry was intact. The U.S. market was large and affluent, and the emerging threat of the Soviet Union led the government to fuel a defense establishment as well as a major research-and-development effort.

These advantages were in addition to the strong positions a number of important industries had established before the war. As Europe recovered, U.S. companies moved in to provide much-needed products—autos, sewing machines, and airplanes were provided by U.S. subsidiaries. The United States produced 80 percent of the world's automobiles and 50 percent of its steel.

During the 1950s and 1960s, U.S. productivity growth was the highest in the world. U.S. businesses enjoyed unprecedented success during this period, as did U.S. workers who enjoyed the highest wages in the world. With the sometimes exception of Switzerland, American long-term interest rates were the lowest of all industrialized nations well into the 1960s.

During this period, U.S. business became used to easy superiority. In turn, most Americans began to believe in their nation's invulnerability. Second-generation and then third-generation descendants of immigrants lost sight of the challenge that accompanied the American dream. It was all too easy and taken for granted.

Sometime after World War II, the United States lost its edge and its vision. The intellectual foundation on which the nation's economic well-being had been built began to crumble; education became the end game instead of a pathway to work; work became less important than schooling; business meetings became more important than business results; being a manager became more important than managing.

In his seminal study *The Competitive Advantage of Nations*, Michael Porter describes the changes that began occurring to the United States:

> Beginning in the late 1960s, broad segments of American industry began to lose competitive advantage. America's balance in merchandise trade went into deficit for the first time in the twentieth century in 1971. Trade problems widened even though the dollar fell in the latter 1970s. Real wages, after decades of growth, flattened and began declining in 1973. Productivity growth, while long only moderate, became anemic.[10]

Porter goes on to describe the complex and interconnected factors that he believes caused this reversal of fortune. One of these factors was the ability to commercialize technology, which he reports has been adversely affected by the "eroding quality of human resources relative to other nations."[11]

How has this shift in U.S. competitiveness manifested itself? Table 1–1 demonstrates the continuing decline in productivity growth per employee in the United States compared to eight other industrialized nations.[12] From a net creditor position of $141 billion at the beginning of 1982, America shifted to debtor status and by the end of 1986 owed $264 billion.[13] Corporate pretax returns on manufacturing assets averaged 12 percent in 1968 and have fallen to 7 percent.[14] In 1960, foreign inventors received only 20 percent of U.S. patents and now receive nearly 50 percent.[15]

Statistics like these portray the symptoms of America's economic illness, but they do not describe the disease. Real problems in real corporations do. For example in Japan, 19.1

TABLE 1-1
Overall Labor Productivity Growth, 1950–1987[1]
(Compound Annual Growth in Gross Domestic Product per Employee)

Nation	1950–87	1950–55	1955–60	1960–65	1965–70	1970–75	1975–80	1980–85	1985–87
Japan	5.9%[4]	—	6.3%	11.0%	9.2%	3.8%	3.8%	3.0%	2.5%
Korea	5.8%[5]	—	—	—	8.8%	4.6%	4.6%	5.7%	6.6%
Italy	4.4%	6.1%	6.4%	5.7%	6.8%	2.1%	3.0%	1.4%	2.8%
Germany	3.8%	6.4%	5.2%	4.2%	4.4%	2.7%	3.0%	1.9%	1.2%
Denmark	2.4%[4]	—	3.2%	3.5%	3.6%	1.7%	1.7%	1.8%	0.6%
Sweden	2.3%[6]	—	—	4.4%	3.5%	1.7%	0.6%	1.6%	1.7%
United Kingdom	2.2%	2.1%	2.1%	2.4%	2.8%	2.0%	1.7%	2.4%	2.0%
Switzerland	1.2%[7]	—	—	—	—	1.5%	0.7%	1.3%	1.8%
United States	1.4%	2.9%	1.2%	2.5%	0.9%	0.7%	0.5%	1.0%	0.5%

manhours of labor are required to assemble an automobile. At Japanese auto plants in the United States, 19.5 manhours are expended building the average car; the average number of assembly hours for a car manufactured in U.S. auto plants is 26.5.[16] Motorola estimates that the training expense in Japan for a process similar to one that Motorola uses is about $1—the cost of a manual that new employees study at home. Motorola's cost was running between $200 and $2,000, depending on how much time was necessary to spend on remedial reading—Motorola had to put workers in classrooms for weeks to achieve the same level of understanding as their Japanese counterparts.[17] IBM plants in Japan producing the same products as their U.S. counterparts frequently outperform them when it comes to yields, turnaround times, development-cycle times, and costs.[18]

Although the United States is still the most productive country in the world, our lead is being whittled away because of declining productivity, which is due importantly to unsatisfactory levels of educational and skill attainment. C. Jackson Grayson and Carla O'Dell predict in their book *A Two-Minute Warning* that if current levels of productivity growth continue, the United States will rank eighth among industrialized nations by early in the next century—behind France, Norway, Germany, Belgium, Canada, Japan, and Italy.[19]

The American standard of living has begun to decline. Although there are winners and losers in the diverse economy of the United States, on average, the trends are in the wrong direction. Robert Z. Lawrence, an economist at the Brookings Institution, estimates that during the 1990s, the standard of living in the United States will decline about 3 percent, wiping out the gains of the 1980s.[20]

Anecdotally, nearly everyone has a story to tell about the child who returned home to live because he or she could not support themselves, about the young married couple who couldn't afford to buy a house even with two incomes, or about layoffs.

The United States is undergoing a profound metamorphosis, a change that is accelerating the success and wealth of some people while lowering the standards of living of others—

roughly, the more educated you are, the wealthier you are. And the disparities are not just based on racial discrimination. Undereducated white youths are having trouble finding worthwhile work. Nor are they just based on inner city versus rural conditions—corporations are slimming all over the United States, and white-collar workers are not a lot safer than blue-collar workers.

Although the United States has emphasized the importance of education throughout most of its history and has reaped the rewards of superior productivity, it has lost ground during the past several decades because of differences in national motivation between this country and others.

As the most egalitarian society, the United States has provided educational opportunities for its youth because as a nation we have believed that education is the foundation required for *individual* ambitions and *individual* success. We are a nation of individual accomplishment, where the sons and daughters of poor farmers and immigrants could bootstrap themselves into business and other success. Our history is replete with Horatio Alger stories—we revere those who made their way on their own.

Other nations have a cultural tradition of group, or national, ambition. These nations provide education to improve the *national* wealth and the *national* business posture. Accordingly, there is national consensus within our industrialized competitors regarding the importance of education as it affects work, careers, and their standards of living. The effect of these differing motivations for educating youth has helped these other nations and hurt the United States, particularly as the New Global Commercial System has evolved.

As worker knowledge and training have become more important factors in determining national comparative advantage—and as natural resources, capital, distance, and technology have subsided in importance to international trade—this national consensus in other countries has led to worker-oriented programs that are the foundation of development of the new business paradigm. This has not happened in the United States. The U.S. education system has not shifted. The

United States has not developed the public policies needed to increase the productivity of its workers. Business has coasted on the stream of post-war superiority.

Although U.S. manufacturers have improved productivity during the past several years, they remain vulnerable to more efficient foreign producers. The service sector of the U.S. economy—now over 70 percent of the total—experienced actual declines in productivity in 1989 and 1990.[21]

Much is written about productivity, and business certainly is interested in improving it, but more attention needs to be paid to the linkage between national productivity and the nation's standard of living. Viewed on a per capita basis, productivity and individual wealth are more easily understood.

A nation can achieve *per capita* improvements in its standard of living in only three ways: by increasing the percentage of people working and, therefore, the amount of output; by workers working longer hours; and by increasing the amount of output per worker.

All of these events are occurring daily in a country's commercial environment. During the past decade, women and teenagers increased their participation in America's workforce significantly. Immigrants joined the workforce. As the economy boomed, unemployment rates dropped, and average hours worked per week rose. Combined with the high levels of debt Americans burdened themselves with, these productivity inputs fueled the longest economic expansion in our history.

Despite this fortuitous activity, annual business productivity growth in the United States during the 1980s averaged an anemic .9 percent.[22] The result was a decline in the standards of living for many Americans. Families with two incomes managed to keep even with inflation, but during the 1980s the highest earning one third of the population realized all the economic gains.[23]

The future possibilities don't appear bright for a quick turnaround to this situation. The Conference Board projects that for Americans to increase their standards of living by just 1.5 percent per year over the next decade, business productivity must increase at a rate of 1.2 percent annually during the same period.[24]

Their reasoning is that the number of 16-year-olds entering the U.S. workforce will increase annually only by about .9 percent, and that other participation in the workforce will increase only about .3 percent each year (women entering the workforce). This means that we cannot depend on new workers to increase output at a rate that will outstrip inflation. In addition to adding these new workers to the workforce, we must achieve that 1.2 percent in business productivity through higher output from the other workers.

There is little evidence that U.S. companies can increase productivity growth from the .9 percent it achieved during the "boom" years of the 1980s to the 1.2 percent we need in the 1990s. Unless business drastically revises the way it operates, the standard of living in the United States will decline dramatically. Moreover, the "pie" will continue to be divided more unevenly, with exaggerated declines in the lower portion of the economic ladder in this country.

The effects of these trends are already apparent, but there has not yet been enough public discussion to cause a national consensus and a resolve to change public policy and private-sector operations.

Knowledge work is a mixed picture in the United States, with college graduates continuing to compete fairly well with their international counterparts. The problem is, the other 75 percent of the nation's population is falling further and further behind.[25]

In other nations, knowledge workers are defined quite differently and include a greater percentage of the population. Apprenticeships, vocation, and skills training are considered as important as college degrees in many of these nations. Unfortunately, in the United States the misguided notion that only advanced education is worthwhile has turned into a self-fulfilling prophesy.

Who are America's frontline workers? There are a number of ways to categorize workers in the United States. The Commission on the Skills of the American Workforce estimates that about a third of business jobs require a college degree; about a third, a high school diploma; and the remainder a 10th grade education.[26]

Robert Reich categorizes business workers as symbolic analysts (college graduates) at 33 percent, routine production workers at 40 percent, and in-person service workers at 27 percent.[27] He draws the distinctions in this manner in order to identify those workers who must compete for their jobs on an international basis. He argues that only in-person service workers don't compete because their physical presence is required in the United States (i.e., have transactions directly with customers).

Higher-level U.S. managers and executives, scientists, engineers, financial brokers, lawyers, and other professional workers—knowledge workers—are paid well and can compete with the best in the world. However, frontline workers in U.S. manufacturing and service industries have been short-changed. Because of the tumbling barriers to international business, many of these American workers must now compete on a worldwide basis for their jobs. And they are caught in the middle.

Data-entry personnel paid $7 per hour cannot compete with English-speaking data-entry workers in India who will work for $2 a day, and the raw data can be in Delhi overnight and returned via satellite.

Processors of insurance forms expecting $10 per hour are being laid off because the same work is now done in Ireland and the Barbados for half the cost. PC keyboards can be assembled in Singapore for one fifth the cost as in the United States.

And low-cost, low-skill jobs are not the only jobs at risk. German manufacturers can afford to pay skilled machine tool operators $2 more per hour than their U.S. counterparts because the German operators have the training and education that allows them to do the same tasks as U.S. numerically controlled operators, plus their supervisors, plus the maintenance crew. Automobile workers in some nations are paid more than their U.S. counterparts because fewer of them can produce better-quality cars than are produced in the United States.

The international competition for jobs—either low-wage or high-wage—is just beginning. American businesses are just starting to operate on a global basis, and foreign producers are just beginning to tap the U.S. market. The problem is that U.S. businesses and their workers are starting the race one lap late.

Other nations are up and running with a well-educated and a well-trained workforce, and unskilled workers are losing whatever leverage they have in the workforce.

For example, in 1960, 35 percent of non-farm workers belonged to labor unions. In 1990, only 17 percent were union members.[28] In 1949, wages of production workers accounted for 11.6 percent of the nation's gross national product, and by 1990 it had fallen to 4.6 percent.[29] The balance of costs are now consumed by designers, planners, and other white-collar knowledge workers in both manufacturing and service industries.

The BFGoodrich Company is developing desktop manufacturing technology that will produce wax or plastic prototype parts in hours instead of weeks. The technology allows an engineer to design a part on a computer screen. When the engineer is satisfied with the image (or has reproduced an engineering drawing), he then orders a laser beam to reproduce the part by sintering powered wax or plastic. Driven by the computer, the laser beam shapes the material into the three-dimensional figure. This operation can be repeated over and over in a few hours until the part is completed. The process could yield a significant reduction in time-to-market for many new products.

This sort of advancement in basic manufacturing calls into question the categories of skills currently measured by government agencies and economists. In this example, skilled model makers are eliminated because there is no need to build a mold; workers involved with converting the mold into a finished part are eliminated. Craftsmen who for decades have produced model parts for manufacture on machine tools can be replaced by technicians who can be taught to operate a computer keyboard, or a mouse. The process allows knowledge workers to skip several phases of production, or to actually do the work themselves.

Of course, in many new industries, such as the computer industry, the percentage of knowledge-worker costs is even greater than in the modern manufacturing plant—Tandy reports that manufacturing labor costs are only 2 percent of its costs to product a PC.[30] In many service industries, such as advertising and publishing, knowledge workers occupy nearly all the chairs—the assets go home every evening.

The United States has done a good job of remaining competitive in industries that depend for the most part on individual workers with a high degree of knowledge. In fact, foreign companies tend to focus on these sorts of businesses when they seek acquisitions in this country. Although many people fret about foreign ownership of these U.S. companies, they should remind themselves that the truly valuable assets that foreign companies seek are the talent, knowledge, and skills of employees—assets that can't be exported and that can change jobs if not satisfied.

The principal problem with U.S. business, however, and the reason that the United States is realizing smaller pieces of the global commercial pie, is that we have not been able to transfer the notion of knowledge-work into the frontline sectors of our manufacturing and service industries. For some reason, we value thinking and education only down through a certain level in our organizations. Beyond that, we continue to organize along the mass production, standardized-product model, developed early in this century, which requires everyone to think except the frontline worker.

It has been said that women are frustrated by a glass ceiling that bars advancement; frontline workers confront a sieve ceiling that allows them to know a little bit about their jobs but not the whole story!

The social and financial toll we are paying for this attitude is enormous. Many U.S. businesses are frantically searching for low-cost workers so they can lower production costs. Others are further simplifying work to accommodate worker-skill levels. Ultimately, this is a failed strategy. Workers in many other countries are paid less than our low-wage workers, and eventually their output will be imported into the United States. In some countries, workers are better trained and can deliver better productivity through more-efficient work environments.

If this situation is permitted to worsen—if U.S. businesses are squeezed between low-wage producers and high-productivity producers—many U.S. companies will either be driven out of business in the coming decade or will be forced to take their production offshore. If a sizable number of U.S. workers lose their jobs or continue to receive lower wages, the American economy will deteriorate.

The systems that require repair in order to reverse this situation are huge. Only a concerted effort of national will, with cooperation at all levels, will slow the deterioration and then begin the recovery. To obtain this will and to go to work on solutions, the U.S. business community must lead the effort to energize the public and our elected officials.

The workforce problem the United States faces can be separated into three parts:

1. The nation's education system is no longer competitive with other countries.
2. The United States does not prepare new workers for jobs and it does not train current workers nearly enough.
3. U.S. business is not organized in a manner to take advantage of skilled workers.

These three sectors of the American terrain are very large and complex—rooted in traditions and entwined with vested interests. Although there is some recognition by business people that they have to be torn apart and then reassembled, there continues to be a great deal of reluctance to do so. For example, U.S. businesses have undergone a traumatic restructuring that has resulted in a fair amount of decentralization and searching for new solutions for the 1990s. Even so, few companies have transferred power below the division-manager level or plant-manager level. There is still not enough recognition by business managers that frontline workers must have a role in upgrading the profitability of the enterprise.

By the same token, relatively little effort has been made to include school teachers in the education reform process. Most of the effort to date has been at the state level or, at best, at the school district level.

Additionally, Americans still cling to the idea that blue-collar work, even highly skilled work, manifests some sort of social failure. Despite the fact that only about a third of the jobs in the United States require college degrees,[31] most parents want their children to attend college, and about 50 percent do so.[32] Consequently, there is little agitation for training and placement systems leading to highly paid noncollege work.

The current environment in the United States is self-destructive. These systems must be altered, and the U.S. business community must take a leadership role in advocating and implementing change.

CHAPTER 2

THE WORK-ORGANIZATION
GAP

It's not possible to calculate the effects of work-organization differences among nations. There is compelling anecdotal evidence, however, that the principal difference between productivity growth in the United States compared to its industrialized competitors is the inefficiencies of the American style of organization. Other nations are realizing more output per worker, and the differences are not due to longer working hours or greater automation.

For example, the General Motors-Toyota joint-venture plant in Fremont, California, is 40 percent more productive than the average of other GM plants.[1] The United Auto Workers agreed to reduce the number of job classifications in the plant so that workers could undertake a variety of activities on a team basis.[2] Over 200 production workers spent three weeks at Toyota's Japanese plants learning the Japanese approach to production.[3] These core workers then trained 2,000 of their U.S. coworkers.[4]

Caterpillar, which lost over $1 billion in the mid–1980s, massively restructured its entire approach to manufacturing.[5] Included in this change was adoption of a "just-in-time" system, a 75-percent reduction in job classifications, formation of work groups, and a reduction in the number of shop floor supervisors.[6] This massive restructuring has led to innumerable improvements, such as assembling transmissions at its Peoria plant in three days instead of three months.[7]

Motorola revamped the way it produces microprocessors at its Austin plant and calculates that it is now competitive with any plant in the world producing similar products.[8] U.S. jobs have been saved. Among the large number of changes at the plant was formation of work teams. There are no foremen, just group leaders, who are hourly employees that have taken over the responsibilities of supervisors.

Not enough U.S. companies have reordered the way work is performed so as to take advantage of technology and to compete with companies from other countries that have done so. A 1990 study by Towers Perrin and the Hudson Institute indicates that only 13 percent of U.S. companies were utilizing self-managed work groups somewhere in their companies.[9] In considering the total U.S. business scene, this percentage is probably too high because only larger firms were queried in this study.

Too many U.S. companies continue to believe that productivity improvements will be realized the old-fashioned way—through capital investments—rather than through the new way—worker training and work reorganization.

An example of this is the record of General Motors during the 1980s, when Ford and Chrysler attempted to upgrade quality and productivity through greater employee involvement.[10] The accompanying table—compiled by the Congressional Office of Technology Assessment and Beier/Gearhart—indicates that although GM invested at a competitive rate during the decade, it did not realize a competitive rate of productivity improvement.[11]

TABLE 2–1
Investment by U.S. Automobile Producers and Productivity Improvement, 1979–89

	General Motors	Ford	Chrysler
Investment in plant and equipment (billions of dollars) .	$72.6[a]	$41.2	$22.5
Investment per vehicle produced	$920[a]	$680	$1,090
Change in labor productivity:			
Engines	13%	43%	9%
Stamping	14	45	30
Vehicle assembly	5	31	19

[a]1979–1988.

Sources: Investment—annual reports. Productivity—Bruce Beier and Mary Gearhart, "Productivity Vs. Profit Sharing," *Automotive Industries*, April 1990, pp. 53–56, based on *The Harbour Report: A Decade Later.*

There has been a fundamental shift in the manner in which goods and services are produced in nations around the globe. Unfortunately, the United States is years behind other countries in understanding the significance of these new approaches and in implementing them. As U.S. business is beginning to understand the value of these techniques, particularly as they apply to improving the quality of products, it is running into a stone wall erected during the past two decades. The stalled U.S. education system and the lack of a skills-training system in the United States have filled U.S. factories and stores with employees who are not capable of operating in the new work environment without significant and expensive remedial training.

In 1911, Frederick W. Taylor published *The Principles of Scientific Management*, and business in the United States has operated on these principles ever since. In fact, most of American society is organized into hierarchical levels with work segmented into parts and people assigned to the parts according to ability. It was once a sensible way to organize factories, hospitals, schools, and other institutions.

Taylor's system called for very specific divisions of work, with laborers doing nothing more than repetitive, physical assembly. It was the right system for the standardized, mass production needs of its time, but it is the wrong system for today.

The reason that the Taylor model of work organization has become dangerous to the health of U.S. business is that it requires too many people to get the job done. Planners, supervisors, factory-floor specialists, maintenance workers, quality-control inspectors, stockroom workers, parts-delivery people—a host of workers are needed, each doing his or her specialized job according to his or her talents.

This abundant approach to work is no longer appropriate for the United States because we have become a high-wage nation. Even our low-wage population is high wage when compared to many other countries. Average U.S. wages are five times higher than wages in Korea and Singapore.[12]

And with the barriers to international business operations tumbling, many of our workers are not competing with these relatively low-wage counterparts. Accordingly, over 700 U.S.

companies already employ over 350,000 people in Singapore, Taiwan, and Mexico.[13]

But most U.S. companies are not in a position to move jobs offshore, nor is it politically possible for U.S. businesses to displace large numbers of workers because of job exports. What this means is that U.S. companies must determine how its current workforce can add more value to high-value products. In fact, U.S. businesses must produce higher-value products and services if they expect to survive because companies with access to low-wage labor will underprice comparable products produced with high-wage U.S. workers.

The evolving concept of international business runs against the logic we have learned during the past 100 years of mass-produced products. The success of the classic assembly line, as characterized by Charlie Chaplin in *Modern Times*, depended on long runs of standardized products utilizing many employees with narrow responsibilities. (As Henry Ford said, "You can have it in any color as long as it's black.") With the growth of markets over the years, logic would indicate that these mass-production techniques would be in greater demand. In fact, the opposite has occurred.

Today, flexibility, customization, and delivery schedules pace the advanced manufacturing system. Many factories are no longer enslaved to long runs to achieve low unit cost—factory-floor computers and computer-aided design and manufacturing systems now allow efficient short runs. Service companies find that customers require speed, perfection, and personal service. Despite the enormous size of the U.S. market and the world market, we have entered the era of customized mass production of goods and services.

Modern corporations have figured out how to deliver customized products with low unit costs to large numbers of individuals. In the manufacturing sector, this requires that fewer employees than in the past manage the systems that ensure the right parts get to the right assembly point at the right time. It requires that design engineers understand the problems assembly-line employees have. And it requires that product quality be optimized not only to please customers but to reduce costs associated with rework, repair, scrap, and warranties.

In the service sector, customers expect on-time delivery of services at low cost and with a smile. Federal Express trained us to expect overnight delivery; Embassy Suites trained us to expect larger rooms without higher prices; and McDonald's trained us to expect high-quality food at low cost. In all these cases, a new strategy for delivering service was developed, and people were trained to implement it.

Few customers ever see a Federal Express employee, but thousands of them are efficiently operating a new work organization and doing so with commitment and responsibility. Nordstrom's Department store, on the other hand, depends importantly on the enjoyable experience its customers have interfacing with its sales force to sell its products and, with the highest sales-per-square-foot in the industry, has achieved success while paying some sales people as much as $100,000 per year through bonus systems.[14]

In all these cases, companies have adopted a strategy for delivering products and have organized their workforces accordingly. These employees are trained, empowered, and motivated to do their jobs. The result is higher profits, shared in the form of higher wages.

In many other countries, most workers have been empowered to think, reason, plan, report, and take full responsibility for their output. The Taylor model of work is obsolete in these environments because workers have many tasks, not just one. Team, or group, production is the norm in most industrialized nations but not in the United States.

Moreover, accompanying the concept of team work are a number of other systems that improve the efficiency of the workplace. Just-in-time systems, where vendor deliveries are scheduled so that parts are delivered a short time before they are needed, reduce inventory costs but also have broad ramifications for an organization. Parts departments, parts ordering systems, factory-floor delivery personnel, and other aspects of a traditional manufacturing organization are affected.

Perhaps the most profound change in modern manufacturing organizations is the concept of total quality. Originally, the doctrine of quality improvement was preached by pioneers such as Philip Crosby as a straightforward money-saving technique. The idea was that you could save a great deal of expense if you could eliminate or reduce dependence on quality control, inspection, and rework activity in a factory. Although the approach endorsed by Crosby was similar to Edward Demming's Statistical Process Control concept, the approaches differed in implementation because of the varying nature of different manufacturing activity. These concepts have been refined considerably over the years, mostly by the Japanese, and now can be applied to any sort of activity, including white-color staff activity.

The greatest effect of total quality on organization, however, is the effect on line organizations that are interdependent with suppliers and other company organizations. Implemented at the extreme, total quality depends on each organization involved in production and delivery of a product to produce a perfect outcome. If each part of the production and delivery system operates perfectly, the organization can be slimmed considerably.

More importantly, to achieve this sort of perfection, the structure of the organization must be altered because it is much more dependent on frontline workers to operate the system, and less so on supervisors. Management may keep track of outcomes through computer-based reporting systems; but if management builds layers of checkers, orderers, planners, and supervisors into the system, savings will be lost and workers will not exercise responsibility and care.

The first law of total quality is that the more backup built into the system, the greater will be the number of defects: defects will rise to satisfy defect-detection personnel and systems!

Although it is simpler to discuss these new work systems in a manufacturing environment, in service industries, empowered employees are also crossing new borders. In German banks, what we call tellers provide total service to customers, including the granting of loans.[15] They establish relationships with their customers and maintain their business.

In the United States, tellers are low paid, semi-professionals who handle the same responsibilities they have handled for 50 years. Backing them up are supervisors and specialists, each with their individual expertise and, of course, cost.

It's not readily apparent that American workers in service industries are competing for their jobs with foreign workers, but it is obvious that U.S. corporations must become more profitable if they are going to maintain their markets. In the not-too-distant future, international borders will not inhibit even local banking operations. It is possible right now to have on-line banking services through your home computer, so what difference does it make which bank is on the other end of your telephone line?

That the U.S. service sector must upgrade its productivity is clear. At about 70 percent of the U.S. gross domestic product, service industries hold the key to advancing standards of living in this nation.[16] The record is not encouraging to date. Since 1979, the Bureau of Labor Statistics has recorded an average annual increase in service-sector productivity of just .2 percent and an outright decline in 1989 and 1990.[17]

One company that has attacked the service-productivity quandry successfully is United Services Automobile Association, an insurance and investment management company for active and retired armed services personnel.[18] It has substantially increased its assets during the past decade and enjoys a 99 percent renewal rate among customers.[19]

USAA hired the American Productivity and Quality Center in Houston, which is headed by C. Jackson Grayson, to help it devise a quality management system.[20] The system they developed measures the output of every employee in the organization every month and helps management determine bonuses and promotions.[21]

USAA backs up its demands for top-notch customer service with top-notch training: 2.7 percent of payroll annually; good benefits, including four-day, 38-hour weeks and an unusual attention to employee needs on the job; and a 70-year record of no layoffs.[22] Computers empower USAA workers.[23] With one of the most advanced systems in its industry, a USAA service person has a customer's total profile on the screen immediately and is in a position to handle any request for service, from auto and home insurance to a request for information regarding mutual funds.[24]

Interestingly, these labor-saving approaches are paying off even where labor is not a major cost component. According to a study by Bruce Beier and Mary Gearhart, direct labor in the U.S. automobile industry accounts for 10 percent of costs while indirect labor accounts for an additional 15 percent.[25]

At first glance, it would appear that labor couldn't add much to the bottom line in these industries. The principal savings that educated, trained, empowered employees can provide come by way of a multitude of changes an employer can make in the overall process of producing goods and services. Better quality, less scrap, less inventory, less work in process, fewer supervisors—the savings add up quickly. In the case of service industries, on-time delivery, personalized service, customer rapport, and other traits are marketing tools that will reward companies that train their employees.

A number of reasons explain why only a small percentage of U.S. companies have adopted this approach to work organization. Although the concept has been widely reported, some companies have not shifted systems because foreign competitors have not yet arrived at their customers' doorsteps with less expensive goods. Others would like to change but do not have the resources to upgrade the abilities of their present workforce. The primary problem in overcoming the inertia to maintain the status quo in work organization in the United States is the investment needed to improve the abilities of workers so they can accept greater responsibility for their output.

It's been proven that U.S. workers can handle the new work environments—at Honda U.S., at GM Fremont, at Motorola, at IBM, at GE, and at many other companies that are willing to make the necessary investments.

However, unless most U.S. companies adopt new work systems, foreign productivity will continue to outpace U.S. productivity growth. As John Welch, the CEO of the General Electric Company, told *Fortune* magazine,

> We've got to simplify and delegate more—simply trust more. We need to drive self-confidence deep into the organi-

zation. A company can't distribute self-confidence, but it can foster it by removing layers and giving people a chance to win. We have to undo a 100-year-old concept and convince our managers that their role is not to control people and stay "on top" of things, but rather to guide, energize, and excite.[26]

Eighty-five percent of the workforce in the United States in the year 2000 is now working.[27] Thus, U.S. productivity can only improve during this decade through remedial action in the workplace—upgrading of basic academic skills and intensive training. If the education system miraculously improved tomorrow and if there was a school-to-work transition system in place tomorrow, work reorganization would still be needed to save U.S. standards of living.

The ability of a company to create an efficient workplace, however, does not reside entirely in the abilities of its workers. The first priority is for management to adopt a strategic view of the requirements of its markets. What is being sold, to whom, and against what competition? From this strategy will flow requirements for technology, investment, training, and work organization.

A review of the experience of U.S. auto manufacturers as they competed with their Japanese counterparts illustrates the necessity of this strategic beginning.

John Krafcik's study, *Triumph of the Lean Production System*, compares the approaches used by Japanese and U.S. car producers.[28] Krafcik terms the Japanese system as *lean* because it is rooted in a philosophy of avoiding as much work-in-process as possible.[29] The system depends on workers to avoid problems on the manufacturing line rather than correcting them.

Japanese companies have undertaken the risk that an entire production line may be shut down because of an employee mistake. With just-in-time delivery systems and other lean techniques, stopping the assembly line in a Japanese automobile manufacturing plant can idle many workers for a long time.

This approach requires that workers are flexible, knowledgeable, and empowered to make decisions. It also requires a fully integrated process for designing products, including communications between workers on the manufacturing floor and automobile designers. Continuous improvement (Kaisen) work groups and quality circles are important aspects of the system.

In contrast, U.S. automobile production systems depend on backup throughout the cycle—what Krafcik calls "robust" systems.[30] Here, the factory has large inventory buffers in case there is a problem. For the most part, workers are still confined to a routine assembly function, and there is little communication between workers and design engineering.

Lean systems attempt to avoid problems and robust systems attempt to anticipate them. There is little doubt that the lean systems are more productive. Japanese plants in the United States provide more training for workers, achieve better productivity, and produce higher-quality cars.[31]

Design and management of production processes—either manufacturing or services—in other countries depend on worker flexibility and a great degree of independence. In many of these work systems, workers operate in groups and handle activities usually vested in supervisors, maintenance personnel, and other technicians.

In the United States, domestic auto producers typically have 80 to 95 job classifications with strict regulations defining the boundaries between jobs.[32] In U.S. auto plants operated by Japanese producers, there are no more than four classifications with as few as two classifications at some plants.[33] This approach to work provides producers with enormous flexibility and cost savings. Not only are fewer people employed to achieve a specific task, but group members can rotate through various assignments, help one another, and fill in for absent team members.

Additionally, lean systems require (allow) frontline workers to utilize advanced technology, which helps management maintain tighter control of costs. Work reorganization requires workers to input and read data from computers, or computer terminals. This requires additional training. When Martin Marietta installed a computer-based system for production planning and control, it spent five times more on training than it did on hardware and software combined.[34]

The role of computers in business cannot be overemphasized. In 1989, nearly 50 percent of capital expenditures by U.S. companies was spent on computer equipment and software.[35] This startling figure indicates the pervasiveness of computers in the workplace, and to the extent that they are reaching the front lines, frontline workers must be computer-literate. For example, the clerical staff at the Hertz rental car company now use hand-held computers to check in cars in the return lot, and Federal Express delivery people use them to record the disposition of packages. Factory-floor workers use computers to record work completed and to set up computer-controlled machinery.

Computers allow companies to organize work in brand new ways, taking advantage of them to keep track of work in progress and to anticipate the need for replacement parts, new stocks, cars, and replacement people. They allow management to empower employees to an unparalleled degree because management can construct computer-based systems that capture information faster than through a nonautomated human bureaucracy. Thus, as work is decentralized, central control is enhanced because more information is gathered quicker. Unfortunately, U.S. business has given more attention to the use of computers by white-collar workers than it has to the possibilities they offer to make blue-collar workers more productive.

An important difference in the views of management and labor in the United States and in other countries toward work-organization systems is the continuing distrust of many workers and their unions regarding these more cooperative programs. A faction within the United Auto Workers is agitating for a return to confrontational relationships because inherent in these new systems is the need for fewer workers. The International Association of Machinists union has officially condemned work teams and similar activities as no more than a conspiracy of management to gain more control over worker lives.[36]

Business must overcome these views and, where appropriate, convince workers and their representatives that new work systems will produce higher-paying jobs and that large numbers of workers employed in producing products and services is a function of old-fashioned, mass-production systems that are noncompetitive with systems in operation in other countries.

CHAPTER 3

THE TRAINING GAP

America's cultural tradition of self-reliance and rugged individualism has prevented it from undertaking the sort of public/private programs that exist in most industrialized nations for preparing youth for work and for continuous training of adults. In these nations, which also have a long tradition of governmental involvement with private-sector matters, there is strong national consensus for systematic training. This consensus has led to powerful systems that produce expert workers with conscientious and professional work ethics. The result has been to facilitate the adoption of high-performance work environments that, in turn, have led to higher-quality products and more-productive operations.

The systems at work in these nations fall into two categories—school-to-work programs for teenagers and continuous training for adults. A statement of principle by the German Minister of Education and Science in his 1989 report on national vocational and training programs indicates the nature of the formidable competition that U.S. workers confront as they compete for their jobs in the New Global Commerce System.

> The vocational educational policy of the years to come will have to contribute to maintaining and improving the high-qualification level of the labor force as *the most important competitive advantage of the Federal Republic of Germany* as an industrial location.[1] [Italics added]

There are two basic elements to workforce training: a school-to-work system that prepares new workers and continuous training for workers already on the job.

The United States is uncompetitive in both of these areas

compared to most industrialized nations. America does not have a school-to-work system, and few businesses provide enough training to frontline workers to increase their productivity.

In 1988, the Commission on Work, Family, and Citizenship published its report *The Forgotten Half*. The report described America's school-to-work transition system for high school graduates this way: "Noncollege-bound youth who complete high school have been saddled with the thoughtless expectation that they will readily "find their place" and need not be of further concern to the larger society."[2]

Little association exists between the public school system in the United States and the careers of most of its students. Not only have schools failed to provide an internationally competitive standard of learning for basic skills such as reading, writing, and arithmetic, but they are not even organized to help students choose and learn applied skills.

U.S. Bureau of Labor statistics demonstrate the failure of this public attitude in the United States relative to the 50 percent of our youth who never attend college.[3] Table 3-1 shows that the lower you are on the professional ladder, the least likely it is that you received your skills training in college or in high school. For those professions on the bottom of the ladder, what little training has been received came on the job. In no single category of employment in the study did noncollege graduates receive the highest percentage of their training in school.

As with education, there are international comparative tests that indicate the extent of the training gap between U.S. and foreign workers. Since 1950, the International Vocational Training Competition—called the International Youth Skill Olympics (IYSO)—has been held biannually in various countries[4]. Entrants must be younger than 23 and can compete in a variety of categories, ranging from graphic design to welding.[5] In 1989, over 400 people from 21 countries competed.[6]

The United States first entered a team in 1975 and from that year until the 1985 competition, the U.S. team finished last.[7] It was 11th among 18 in 1985, 13th out of 19 two years later, and in 1989, the U.S. team was 13th out of 21.[8]

TABLE 3–1
Sources of Qualifying Training (Percentage of Occupational Group)

Occupational Group	Total with Qualifying Training	From School	Employer-Based	
			Formal	Informal
All employees	55	29	10	26
Professionals	93	82	9	22
Technicians	85	58	14	32
Management-support specialists	77	52	11	38
General managers	71	43	12	39
Craft workers	66	11	16	44
High-tech manufacturing workers	61	17	15	38
Clerical workers	57	33	7	31
Extractive workers	56	4	13	48
Sales workers	43	15	12	28
Machine operators	37	6	6	26
Service workers	36	13	9	18
Transportation workers	36	2	8	26
Laborers	18	2	2	13

Note: For some occupational groups, the percentages add up to more than the total because some employees received training from more than one source.

Source: Carey, Max. Bureau of Labor Statistics, U.S. Department of Labor, *How Workers Get Their Training* (Washington, DC. U.S. Government Printing Office, 1985).

Although the standings of the U.S. teams in these competitions may not accurately reflect the relative skills of the U.S. work force, the IYSO competition does reflect the training policies of various nations. For example, teams from other countries are sponsored by their governments, and the U.S. team is sponsored by a private, nonprofit organization—the Vocational Industrial Clubs of America.[9] In other countries, teams are coached by government agencies and are provided living allowances and prizes.[10]

Korea may be the most intense of the nations entering these competitions. In that country, a payroll levy not only supports vocational institutes, but is also the source of funds for an extensive IYSO awards program. Winners of Korean national skills competitions receive about $9,000 and are certified automatically as Class II craftsmen.[11] Winners of the IYSO receive about $18,000, are exempted from military service, and also are awarded special housing and scholarships.[12] Winners may also start their own businesses using government money.[13] Korea has won seven team titles.[14]

This approach to upgrading the skills of a work force, although exaggerated, typifies national attitudes in most industrialized nations. It stands in stark contrast to U.S. attitudes. In a study of sources of vocational training in the United States, the Bureau of Labor Statistics discovered that most preemployment training is provided by private vocational schools and junior colleges, both of which are paid for by the students.

Public high school vocational training, which was originally designed for students who wished to learn a trade, has become nearly useless for that purpose. Nearly all high school students take at least one vocational course, but only 30 percent of high school students focus on vocational training in preparation for specific occupations.[15] Even so, few graduates from voc-ed courses enter the fields of work for which they studied.[16]

Schools rarely have programs to guide and counsel youth on employment matters. In 1950, the U.S. Employment Service began a job placement service for all high school seniors who were not planning on going to college and offered employment testing and counseling services. By 1963, 600,000 seniors were registered in half of the country's high schools. From that high point, the service has declined to the point where records are no longer kept. Budget cuts and a shift in focus by the Employment Service to disadvantaged people caused the change.

Thus, the United States has by default developed a random system of school-to-work transition that depends nearly entirely on the energy, ambition, and long-range planning interests of youths in the age range of 16 to 25—not a cohort that is noted for its planning ability. The average age of students in community and technical colleges is 29, evidence of the decade of drift we allow our youths to experience.[17] At the most important juncture in their lives for making decisions that will determine their future, their fate, and their fortunes, we have failed to provide basic guidance and training for our youth.

James F. Henry, of the Center for Public Resources, speaking at a national conference on "Functional Literacy and the Workplace," cited the following examples:

> One midwestern financial institution noted that between a third and a half of the high school graduates it decides to hire are unable to complete a math test involving fractions, decimals, and time problems without errors. The results of these deficiencies among employees include incorrect inventories, incorrect reports of production, and improper measurement of machine or parts specifications, with the attendant impact upon product quality and corporate performance. An insurance company informed us that an employee paid a policyholder $2,200 for a dental claim of $100.00 instead of the $22.00 authorized, and did not realize the error.

Business pays the price for this failure every day; as it struggles to find entry-level employees who can handle the most rudimentary work; as it "dummies down" work to accommodate this lack of ability rather than invest in sophisticated technologies that improve productivity. Business also experiences high turnover rates, high accident rates, and high scrap rates resulting from a nonmotivated, nondedicated work force.

Thus, in 1990 as many as 20 million Americans were in their decade of drift—an enormous waste of productive potential. *The Forgotten Half* study also reported the effects of this lack of work preparation on wages. Although real annual earnings dropped for all categories of male employees between the ages of 20 and 24 in the United States between 1973 and 1986, the report found that the percentage of decline rose in accordance with a lack of education—high school dropouts suffered the most with a 42 percent drop.[18]

Education and economic success is a relationship that parents have known about for generations. New elements have entered the equation, however—elements that have aggravated

FIGURE 3–1

Trends in the Real Mean Annual Earnings of 20- to 24-Year-Old Civilian Males, 1973–1986, by Educational Attainment (1986 Dollars)

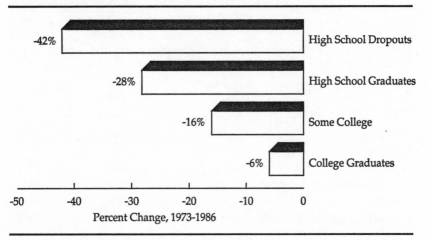

Source: *From School to Work*, a Policy Information Report. Princeton, NJ: Policy Information Center, Educational Testing Service, 1990.

the competitive decline of U.S. business. The new factors are the absence of a school-to-work training system in the United States and the inadequate training U.S. businesses provide its front-line workers.

In the United States, there is no system in place to accommodate those students who need advanced training for the high-skill, high-wage jobs in U.S. business. There is no system for identifying business needs and then providing career guidance and skills training. Nearly all skills training in the United States is on the job and employers are not providing enough of it because workers are not prepared adequately by schools and many employers cannot afford to provide remedial basic education.

In its study, *Workforce 2000*, The Hudson Institute concluded that over half of the new jobs created by the year 2000 would require employees with education beyond the high school level.[19] The Bureau of Labor Statistics (BLS) estimates that these new jobs created in the 1990s will be in knowledge-based industries, with the principal demand for college graduates but with a fair number of noncollege new employees.[20] Just under 50 percent of new jobs generated will be in service areas that can benefit from

TABLE 3–2
Occupations with Greatest Number of New Jobs,1988–2000[a]

	Net Increase in jobs	
	(thousands)	(percent growth)
Retail salespersons	730	19%
Registered nurses	610	39
Custodial workers	560	19
Waiters and waitresses	550	31
Managers	480	16
Office clerks	460	18
Secretaries[b]	380	13
Nursing aides and attendants	380	32
Truck drivers	370	15
Receptionists and information clerks	330	40

[a] BLS moderate growth scenario.
[b] Excludes legal and medical secretaries.

Source: George Silvestri and John Lukasiewicz, "Projections of Occupational Employment, 1988–2000." *Monthly Labor Review*, November 1989, table 6, p. 60.

well-trained employees—retail trade, personal services, whole-sale trade.[21]

The occupations noted in the BLS research with the greatest percentage increases have been traditionally categorized as low-skill positions (see Table 3–2), but a number of them lend themselves to upgrading through effective training.[22] An important test for U.S. business during the next decade is whether it will maintain these positions as low-skill, low-wage jobs or whether it will improve its efficiency by insisting that workers assume more responsiblity.

As new technology, new work organizations, and new products enter the workplace, many jobs are being upgraded. Texas Instruments (TI) now requires that its clean-room personnel in some U.S. plants have two-year technical degrees in addition to high school diplomas.[23] It is not clear whether this requirement was raised because the work became more complex or whether Texas Instruments no longer believes that a high school diploma indicates competence.

In its comparable Japanese facilities, TI uses high school graduates and always introduces new technology in the Japanese facilities before it is introduced in the United States.[24]

A serious training gap exists when measuring the training U.S. workers now receive on their jobs compared to their counterparts in other countries. A report issued in 1990 by the Congressional Office of Technology Assessment concluded: "When measured by international standards, most American workers are not well trained. Many in smaller firms receive no formal training. Our major foreign competitors place much greater emphasis on developing workforce skills at all levels."[25]

When discussing training, there are few standardized measurements. Informal on-the-job training is treated differently than formal schooling, and remedial training in basic skills, such as reading, is also considered training by some companies. Accordingly, it is difficult to compare U.S. expenditures in this area to those in other countries.

The American Society for Training and Development (ASTD) estimates that U.S. companies in the aggregate spend about 1.4 percent of their payroll on training—$44 billion.[26] Like most averages, this estimate is misleading: many small companies conduct no training and others spend as much as 4 or 5 percent of their payroll on training expenses. As indicated earlier, in a number of competitor nations, governmental policies require every company to spend 2 to 4 percent of their payroll costs on training. Combined with better education systems and apprenticeship programs, this training provides a powerful boost to the abilities of these workforces.

Comparisons of the Japanese and American automobile industries, principally through the work of John F. Krafcik, provide a good insight into the differing attitudes regarding worker training.[27] Japanese companies in the United States spend about $1,000 more annually per worker on training than do U.S. companies.[28] Government statistics indicate that Americans working for Japanese manufacturing companies in the United States also earn more than employees of U.S. manufacturing companies— $32,887 versus $28,945 in 1986.

Figures 3–2 and 3–3 demonstrate the approach of Japanese

FIGURE 3–2
Annual Hours of Training per Employee, Automobile Assembly Workers

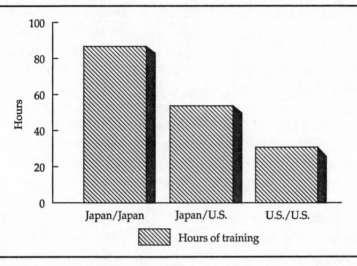

Source: John F. Krafcik, *Training and the Automobile Industry: International Comparisons*, contractor report prepared for the Office of Technology Assessment under contract N3-1910, February 1990, pp. 8–9.

companies and U.S. companies in preparing workers for their responsibilities.[29] The first figure shows that Japanese workers in Japan receive three times as much training each year as U.S. workers in U.S. auto plants. The second figure shows the significant difference in preparation of newly hired workers for their jobs.

To some extent, the difference in training time is accounted for by the differences in work organization employed in Japan and in U.S. auto plants. As discussed in the previous chapter, Japanese workers are given much more responsibility than their U.S. counterparts and, therefore, need additional training.

Perhaps the most serious flaw in U.S. attitudes toward training is the belief that employees other than frontline workers need more of it. The ASTD surveys indicate that salespeople receive the largest amount of training (average hours per individual) followed by first-line managers, middle managers, and other professionals.[30] At the bottom of the list are office/administrative workers and production workers.[31] One encouraging statistic from the latest ASTD survey is the jump in training for pro-

FIGURE 3–3
Hours of Training, Newly Hired Automobile Assembly Workers

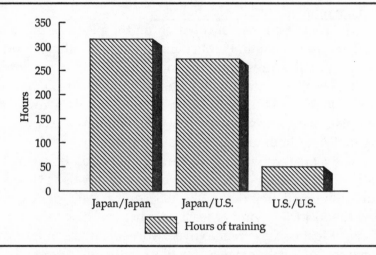

Source: John F. Krafcik, *Training and the Automobile Industry: International Comparisons*, contractor report prepared for the Office of Technology Assessment under contract N3-1910, February 1990, pp. 8–9.

duction workers, probably the result of a growing interest in total-quality systems.[32]

And, according to *Fortune* magazine, executive training rose in 1991 despite a mediocre year for profits.[33] The number of executives attending business-related programs at U.S. colleges rose 10 percent this year.[34] It costs $4,500 per person to attend Columbia University's course on managing a diverse workforce; $12,500 per person to attend Northwestern's four-week business school course; and $15,000 per day for custom-designed courses at Wharton related to "managing shareholder value."[35]

The aggregate number of employees who receive training each year in the United States is about 40 million, one third of the workforce.[36] Unfortunately, younger workers who most need training are least likely to receive it on the job. In a 1983 study by the Department of Labor, 55 percent of all workers reported that they needed some sort of training to qualify for the jobs they held at that time.[37] Of this group, only 14 percent of workers between the ages of 16 and 24 said they had received any training.[38]

A number of studies show that employees who receive training earn higher wages—on average, 10 to 30 percent more—and are more likely to hold their jobs.

The Wall Street Journal reported on the plight of one set of workers from Wyandott, Michigan, who were thrown out of work when the Firestone Tire and Rubber Company closed a plant there that manufactured wheels.[39] Unskilled laborers who made $10.50 to $14.00 an hour found themselves unemployable except for part-time work and low wages.[40] Many are now working for $7 per hour and glad to have the jobs.[41]

The *Journal* reported that during the period between 1981 and 1985, 2.6 million factory workers lost their jobs as U.S. companies slimmed their ranks.[42] By 1986, only 800,000 of this group had found jobs paying at least as much as their former positions.[43] Most of these reemployed workers had been trained at some sort of a skill that was of value to other employers.[44]

That U.S. companies have a dilemma regarding training is without debate. Too many firms find that the basic skills levels of their employees and of prospective employees are so low that they confront two stages of training: remedial training to improve reading, writing, math, and reasoning skills; and specific training to upgrade job productivity. For instance, an Illinois company had to provide remedial training for its Hispanic employees after one of them ruined an $8,000 part because of a language misunderstanding.[45] A Florida company estimates its manufacturing costs are $1.2 million higher because employees can't read blueprints correctly.[46] When Plumley Company, an auto parts supplier in Tennessee, tried to improve its quality control through a statistical process control system, it discovered that nearly half of its 500 workers had not completed high school and that many employees—including supervisors—could not read.[47]

Estimates vary considerably on the amount of remedial training being offered by U.S. businesses, with Society of Human Resource Management surveys indicating 26 percent doing so and American Management Association surveys indicating only 3 percent.[48]

Can U.S. companies afford to spend billions on overcoming

the problems associated with employing undereducated people? Many of those who choose to upgrade their workforces through a modern training regimen will discover that they first must upgrade their employees to the point that they can comprehend the training.

U.S. business has no choice. It must develop a world class workforce if it is to compete and if it is to maintain high standards of living in this country. The appropriate long-range strategy is to train the workforce so that it can operate in high-performance work environments that improve profits and competitiveness through efficiency and high-quality products.

THE PUBLIC-POLICY TRAINING GAP

A country-by-country review of workforce training systems in several competitor nations indicates the disparity between the United States and these countries regarding the perceived importance of the subject.

Federal Republic of Germany. In 1950, West Germany enacted into law the Federal Youth Plan.[49] The Youth Plan covers young people aged 14 to 21 and includes both schooling and vocational education.[50] It complements a public schooling policy that produces a high degree of accomplishment regardless of the direction students take.

School in Germany is required between the ages of 6 and 18 and is the responsibility of the states, just like in the United States.[51] But decentralization of education is the only common characteristic of the two nations' systems. Students who do not go on to college attend school in Germany full time for at least nine years and then part time for two or three additional years, depending on which apprenticeship program they enter.[52] In Germany, this career process begins at age 10, when students take a national examination to qualify for one of three types of schools, each of which starts them down a particular path.[53] Junior high school in Germany lasts eight years and prepares students for an occupation.[54] Intermediate school prepares students for highly skilled work. Grammar school prepares students for college.

The Federal Youth Plan marries education with skills training. Over 70 percent of German youths—both male and female—have received vocational and trade training in the Youth Plan.[55] Typically, after completing school at age 18, a student attends a specialized school one day of the week and receives on-the-job training with a German firm the other four days.[56] Even that one day in school is devoted mostly to trade-oriented studies. This regimen is pursued for two or three years, at which point students take a state-approved examination that qualifies them to pursue their chosen craft or trade.[57]

Business plays a significant role in implementing this system. It provides jobs during the apprenticeship period, it provides on-the-job training, and it subsidizes much of the classroom training. Large companies have their own vocational schools, which are licensed by the state.[58]

Germany's labor-market policies are administered by the states through a system of employment offices at the local labor-market area level. As in the case of the school-to-work transition, business is a full partner with government in the administration of labor-market policy. At each level—national, state, and local—the Federal Employment Agency is controlled by a self-governing body in which associations of employers, unions, and the government are equal partners. The agencies have broad responsibility for providing counseling, placement, training referral, unemployment insurance, vocational rehabilitation, and labor-market information services for workers and employers in all of Germany's labor-market areas.

In 1987, there were 1.8 million participants in the country's apprenticeship programs, and German business was spending about $1.5 billion on them.[59] Although German business believes in apprenticeship training, there also is a financial incentive to maintain these programs. In 1976, Germany passed a law that requires all businesses to pay a tax of up to .25 percent of company payroll if in any year the total number of apprenticeship openings is not 12.5 percent above the number of students applying for apprenticeship positions.[60] The tax has never been levied.

Although the government does not provide direct payments to employers for employee training, it does provide an infrastructure employers may utilize. For example, group training centers have been established for small businesses.[61]

Like the United States, Germany has a system for training displaced workers. The Federal Employment Institute offers a number of programs to reduce unemployment, including direct subsidies to employers who provide training that upgrades individual skills.[62]

The German model of school-to-work skills training is based on a culture that tolerates a rigid form of life-style and early life-style decision making, which probably is inappropriate for the United States. The point of the German example, as in many other nations, is that the German public and the German business community have a shared view of work preparation that has resulted in productive policies at all levels of government.

French apprenticeship programs are in an embryo stage. Currently, the programs are viewed as remedial activities for high school dropouts rather than an important school-to-work transition system. Accordingly, only about 15 percent of school attendees are enrolled—220,000 youths.[63] Although this is a low percentage, considering the comparative size of the two nations, it is significant compared to the 300,000 people who are enrolled in U.S. apprenticeship programs each year.[64]

To improve the program, the French government has begun to offer financial incentives to businesses to enlarge apprenticeship programs; for example, employers are exempt from paying social security taxes on apprentice wages.[65]

France requires all employers with more than 10 employees to spend at least 1.2 percent of their payrolls on training.[66] There is an additional payroll tax of .5 percent to support apprenticeship training.[67] If an employer does not spend the minimum amount on training, the balance is paid to the national treasury to support a government-operated training program.[68]

Although it appears that, on average, French businesses exceed the required training expenditure, frontline workers are not receiving much of the benefit. The law does not specify who is to receive the training.[69]

In French firms of all sizes, the amount of training provided is most likely to go to managers and executives first, then technicians, followed by white-collar workers, skilled blue-collar workers, and unskilled blue-collar workers.[70]

Japan does not stress skills training for its youth, principally because it produces such highly educated students able to rely on quick and inexpensive on-the-job learning.[71] In fact, in Japan, university graduates now face declining incomes because there are so many of them compared to available managerial positions. The Japanese work environment does not require a great many supervisors.[72]

Japan has compulsory school for six years of elementary and three years of junior high school.[73] Ninety-four percent of young people continue on to high school for another three years. About 35 percent of high school graduates go directly on to work. Employers hire virtually all of these youths based on the schools' recommendations. About 30 percent of the high school graduates continue on to university, junior college, or technical college, and about 28 percent attend schools outside the regular school system, primarily proprietary schools. Many attending proprietary schools are youths who are not accepted in college and are studying to take the college entry test again. Others are interested in obtaining a specific qualification, such as for a computer programmer. Japanese employers take on much of the responsibility for developing the occupational skills of the workforce. About three-fourths of Japanese firms provide some training to their workers. The main training components provided by the firms are on-the-job training, including rotating workers among assignments; training off the job, such as in centers organized by the firms; correspondence courses; and worker participation in group activities aimed at improving the firm's performance.

Youths in Japan obtain employment almost exclusively through school-employer linkages. High schools are ranked academically within each school district, and students take a high school entrance examination to determine which school they can attend. Each school has ties with employers who assign a certain number of jobs to the school for its graduates. More prestigious employers with better job offers recruit from the higher-ranked schools. Almost all Japanese high school students seeking work are placed in jobs through their schools, and they start work immediately upon graduation. In the beginning of each school year, Japanese high schools, acting as agents of the public employment service, nominate and rank their graduating students for each of the job offers, using grades and behavior as their main criteria. The use of grades as a selection criterion motivates students to do well and helps them realistically assess their career options. The schools know the employer's expectations and nominate students who they think will fulfill them. The employers then interview and hire all or most of the nominees.[74]

United Kingdom.   The United Kingdom is in its third generation of school-to-work systems. In 1964, the Industrial Training Act was implemented with the primary goal of establishing youth apprenticeship programs.[75]

Industrial Training Boards (ITB) were established in each industry with the authority to levy taxes on employers in accordance with the training needs of the industry.[76] Various formulas were implemented and the funds were redistributed back into the industries to support training programs. Most ITBs were disbanded in the early 1980s because they had become ineffective and expensive.[77]

In 1983, the Youth Training Scheme (YTS) was installed in England and has replaced the old apprenticeship system.[78] The government now guarantees a two-year training program for all 16-year-olds and 17-year-olds who leave school.[79] The Youth Training Scheme now has nearly 70 percent of these youth enrolled.[80]

Most apprenticeship training under YTS takes place at the workplace, but 20 weeks of training take place off site.[81] The British government provides an allowance for trainees, who receive a vocational diploma when they complete their program.[82] It is estimated that this program has cut Britain's youth unemployment rate in half.

In a historic change in the management of its employment

and training programs, Great Britain, in 1988, shifted responsibility for the planning and delivery of these youth and adult programs from the government to a new system of local business-led Training and Enterprise Councils (TECs). The TECs were charged with broad responsibility for promoting training of employed workers and assisting in small business development.

This radical transformation in the governance structure from a centralized, government-administered series of independent programs to locally based, private sector-managed integrated systems reflects, as did the older partnership arrangements in Germany and Sweden, a business-government consensus about the critical importance of the nation's human capital. As the government White Paper, Employment for the 1990s, indicated in establishing the TECs:

> By any measure there is a need for radical reform of our training system. We need to recognize the commercial necessity of reskilling people, and the central importance of linking training plans with business plans. What is now needed is a new framework for training and enterprise. . . . The Government's aim is to promote, in a new partnership with employers, the establishment of such a training system—one which will be capable of contributing much more effectively to Britain's international competitive success. The aim must be to facilitate access to relevant training and vocational education throughout working life for every member of the work force, at every level from entry to top management.[83]

Beginning in 1989 and over a period of three to four years, 100 TECs will be established throughout the country. Two of the guiding principles of the TECs are that they must have a local focus and be business led. The initiative for the creation of a TEC must come from the local community. Initial applications and detailed business plans are submitted by local business and community leadership for approval by both the Secretary of State for Employment, acting for the government, and a National Training Task Force, representing the nation's business leaders.

TECs are clearly under the direction of local business—at least two thirds of a TEC's board of directors, including the chairperson, must be from the private sector—and, to ensure the quality of that membership, the business members must be either the chairpersons or chief executives of their firms. In the case of major companies, the senior operational local manager qualifies. The remaining TEC members may be chief executives of local labor, education, volunteer, or other organizations.

The scope of the TECs' responsibility is impressive. They have responsibility for current employment and training programs and have broad flexibility to integrate these programs into coherent plans of action designed to meet local needs. In addition, the TECs are further encouraged to go beyond existing government programs to meet the community's broader training and business development requirements. Specifically, the TECs are charged with these responsibilities:

- Examining the local labor market, assessing key skill needs, prospects for expanded job growth, and the adequacy of existing training opportunities.
- Drawing up a plan, with measurable objectives, to provide or secure quality training and enterprise development to meet these needs.
- Under the plan, tailoring and managing government training programs for young people, for the unemployed, and for individuals needing technical retraining, as well as providing training and other support for small businesses.
- Promoting and directing increased private sector investment in training, vocational education, and enterprise activities designed to strengthen the local skill base and to spur economic growth.

Basic funding for the TECs is provided by the government under performance contracts. As independent companies, TECs have the authority to raise additional public and private funds to widen the scope of their operations.

Norway, Sweden, and Ireland have some form of government/private skills training system. Norway offers a combination of academic and vocational training right in the schools for students between the ages of 16 and 18.[84]

Ireland, with a third of its unemployed under age 25, recognizes the importance of youth training and has established a one-percent Youth Employment Levy on all personal income.[85] In 1983, the National Youth Policy Committee was established to develop a national youth policy.[86]

Sweden has a youth-unemployment problem and the country has taken steps to reverse the situation. Counselors begin to provide information about various careers to students in the sixth grade, and students spend 6 to 10 weeks observing various occupations in the workplace.[87]

Swedish companies must deposit part of their pretax profits in a national account that can be used only for training and for R&D.[88] Finally, Sweden has a national curriculum that includes emphasis on linking theoretical learning with practical application in the work environment.[89]

Singapore has an extensive training regime. Employers must pay a levy of 1.0 percent of the aggregate payroll of employees earning less than $750 (U.S.) per month into a national Skills Development Fund—essentially, a tax on unskilled workers.[90]

Employers can escape the tax by paying higher wages or by convincing the government that their training programs will significantly increase the skills of their workers. If the government accepts a training program, the employer gets his tax back plus a bonus.[91]

Additionally, Singapore has a federal apprenticeship program and a National Training Award Scheme for employers who have outstanding programs—a counterpart to the Malcolm Baldrige Awards for U.S. companies that produce superior products and service in the United States.[92]

Table 3–3, compiled by the OECD, compares the spending and participation rates for labor-market programs of six industrialized nations. The comparisons indicate the difference in importance the U.S. government places on training compared to competitor nations. Although the U.S. private sector probably prefers to retain control of all employee training, school-to-work systems could be subsidized by federal and state government through high schools and two-year colleges.

Each of these countries seeks some structured fashion to

TABLE 3–3
Participation in Programs Aiming to Promote Permanent Employment: Persons Starting Per Year as Percent of the Labor Force

	France	Germany[1]	Japan	Sweden	United Kingdom	United States
Training for unemployed adults, etc.	2.14%	1.48%	0.17%	1.70%	1.97%	1.02%[2]
Training for employed adults	1.99	—	0.66	0.47	0.38	—
Subsidized apprenticeships and related training	3.32	0.48 [2.11]	—	—	1.43	0.08
Measures for unemployed and disadvantaged youth	1.33	0.40	—	0.60	0.02	0.63
Subsidies to regular private employment, including self-employment	0.39	0.66	—	0.41	0.37	0.49
Rehabilitation and recruitment subsidies for the disabled	—	4.03	—	0.61	0.06	0.75
Total	9.17%	[6.14%]	0.83%	3.79%	4.23%	2.96%
Total measures for the unemployed and disadvantaged	3.86	2.75	0.17	3.33	2.42	2.89

Note: Data refer to the most recent year for which data are available, in most cases 1988.
[1]The main German figures refer to allowances paid in certain cases: the figures within square brackets represent all participants in the apprenticeship system.
[2]Certain relatively large programs have been omitted due to lack of data.

Source: OECD (1990). Scherer, Peter. A Review of National Labour Market Policies in OECD Countries. OECD. Presented at World Bank Seminar on Economic Adjustment: Employment and Social Dimensions. February 1990.

smooth the transition from school to work by giving students occupational information and guidance while in school, by combining schooling with work experience and on-the-job training, and by offering job-placement assistance. The schools themselves systematically facilitate the student's transition from school to work. Employers play a significant role in a youth's transition to work. Most countries provide structured work experience for secondary school students, apprenticeships for most youth in Germany, and formal school-employer linkages for job placement for most youth in Japan. Some countries seek to maintain quality occupational training by testing and certification to meet national standards. Participants who pass competency tests receive nationally recognized credentials, which employers look to as evidence of skill levels of potential hires. The countries generally provide extensive assistance to jobless youth. The programs vary, but reflect a national policy that youth who are unable to gain employment should be given further preparation so that they can become better-qualified workers.

Each of these approaches in foreign countries appears to be rooted in a national judgment that a well-prepared young workforce is vital for national economic performance and international competitive ability. These nations have developed literacy of a relatively high level for all students. The roles and relationships of the schools, public employment agencies, and employers, while differing in each country, tend to be integrated and clear. Thus, most youths know where to turn, and relatively few fall between the cracks in the path from school to work. For youths who do encounter employment difficulty after leaving school, the countries' systems seek to reach most of them. Typically, the assistance is intensive and long term.

Each of these competitive societies, with the exception of Japan, has evolved a rational public policy response to workforce preparation and established the necessary systems of public and private institutions to deliver, coordinate, and certify the training. In the United States, the public responsibility for education and training ends upon leaving high school, and further training in any profession or in a college track is left to individual initiative, and even that success is dependent largely on an individual's access to resources. We provide no systematic assistance for the school-to-work transition, and very little institutional opportunity other than vocational, technical, or community college-level training for those who do not go on to college.

Businesses in competitor nations follow up on these worker-preparation programs with continuous training, sometimes with governmental incentives. Human resource development and maintenance is pervasive in these nations because these societies have decided that worker productivity is a comparative advantage.

U.S. business cannot long ignore the skill-training trends developing in these countries. It is national policy, based on national consensus in these nations to build solid bridges between school and work. Skill training is considered to be as important as education in all industrialized nations except Japan, where education and character are combined to produce skill. U.S. business must lead the effort in the United States to build consensus and then the training infrastructure that will produce students who are better prepared for work.

By the same token, it is unrealistic to expect that the United States can simply clone one of the European systems. In an egalitarian country such as ours, a rigid, life-setting choice at a young age would not be acceptable. Additionally, although the European models produce highly trained new workers, they lack a certain degree of flexibility that truly knowledge-rich employees need for maximum effectiveness.

Thus, the United States must develop a unique system of ensuring that as many new workers as possible can be employed in high-skill, high-wage jobs. In later chapters, we will describe some of the possibilities, but it is certain that this gap will not be closed unless the business community demands change in human-resource public policies.

CHAPTER 4

THE EDUCATION GAP

A nation cannot have a first-place economy with a second-rate education system.

This lesson has been taught repeatedly throughout history. Tracing the parallels in economic growth and educational progress, C. Jackson Grayson, Jr. and Carla O'Dell remind us of the history of Germany, England, and the United States. Frederick the Great made education compulsory for all citizens of Prussia in 1760, and by 1860, 97 percent of school-age children attended classes.[1] In the United States, Massachusetts led the way with compulsory education in 1852, and over the years, the other states followed; the last to do so was Mississippi in 1918.[2]

In England, however, only about half of school-age children attended school in 1860.[3] For years, education in England was considered proper only for the wealthiest portion of the population, and by the turn of the century fewer than 10 percent of children attending school came from poorer families.[4] The results are also reflected in a comparison of German and English university attendance. In 1913, England had 9,000 college students and Germany had 60,000.[5]

Grayson and O'Dell also remind us that in 1870, England was the most productive and richest nation on earth, and by 1986, its standard of living had slipped to ninth place.[6]

It can't be proven that England's relative economic decline was caused by the relative disparity in the education of its workers, but it certainly had to be an important ingredient.

A more recent example of relative economic shift is, of course, the Japanese. In 1960, Japan's share of world commerce was about 3 percent and is now 10 percent. Japanese productivity was 15 percent of U.S. productivity 30 years ago and is now

70 percent and still rising.[7] With a significant cultural focus on education and modern work systems, Japan has built a powerful business system without dependence on natural resources.

The lesson for the United States in this history is the fact that a nation can slip from economic leadership and a high standard of living to second-class status in less than a century. Clearly, there is a relationship between economic leadership and the ability of a nation to create and utilize new technologies. The completion of this syllogism relates to the ability of a nation's workforce to exploit these new technologies and the contribution of a workforce to increased productivity.

To cure the problem of declining U.S. competitiveness—to close the gap—we must first understand it. One symptom was poignantly described by the Conference Board in its 1990 study of literacy in the U.S. workforce.

> Each morning, more than 10 million American workers wake up in a foreign land. Most were born in America, speak our language, and look and sound like other Americans. But they are not. Many live their entire lives in a single neighborhood. Their capacity to earn a living is limited to simple, often menial tasks in familiar locations. No matter what kind of restaurant they eat in, the menu is in a foreign language. They are severely handicapped, but not by any physical incapacity or mental disorder. They are unable to read.[8]

Literacy in the U.S. workforce takes difference forms. According to a study conducted in 1986 among young adults ages 21 to 25 by the National Assessment of Educational Progress (NAEP), 78 percent of high school graduates could read at an 8th grade level and only 56 percent could read at an 11th grade level.[9] Among those who did not complete high school, 27 percent could read at an 11th grade level, and 54 percent had 8th grade reading skills.[10]

The Bureau of the Census estimated in 1982 that 13 percent of all Americans would fail a basic English-language proficiency test.[11] If accurate, this estimate would place the number of Americans who are functionally illiterate at about 20 million people. The Bureau further estimated that 42 percent of this cohort was unemployed, a startling loss of income for the nation and an appalling social price to pay for ignorance.[12]

TABLE 4-1
Percentage of Young Adult Population at or above Average Reading Proficiency

Grade Level	0–8 Years	Level of Education 9–12 No Diploma	H.S. Diploma
11	15.1%	27.4%	55.9%
8	37.0	53.6	77.9
4	73.3	76.1	94.7

Source: *From School to Work*, a Policy Information Report. Princeton, NJ: Policy Information Center, Educational Testing Service, 1990.

The cost to business in lost time, poor performance, and higher personnel costs resulting from employing people with basic skill deficiencies is staggering. A study in the Atlanta Metropolitan Statistical Area by the National Alliance of Business indicates that employees with literacy limitations cost employers $840 million annually—$3,700 per employee.[13] According to the U.S. Department of Labor, the cost of functional illiteracy to employers in eight southeastern states employing 3.6 million undereducated workers is $24.8 billion annually.[14]

The nation's knowledge problem begins with the basics. Even most of those who are ostensibly qualified to fill 85 percent of the country's jobs—high school graduates—can't read as well as their diplomas indicate.[15] If the solution to this problem were as simple as reducing the complexity of written manuals and other forms of training, business might get by, but the inability of workers to read well points to a more serious problem.

The inability to read accompanies an inability to reason and to communicate with others. It just isn't possible to empower workers with decisions and team activities without some level of comparable higher-order skills. Business can't operate effectively at the lowest common denominator of reading and reasoning ability.

In the first statewide test of adult literacy, Oregon reported in 1991 that although 97 percent of its residents can read at some level, an appalling number of them cannot apply that literacy in a practical manner.[16] The Educational Testing Service (ETS) developed this assessment system and will conduct nationwide tests in 1992 to determine how well Americans can use their reading ability to perform routine daily tasks.[17]

In Oregon, it was discovered that 78 percent of the people could read at a basic level, but only 35 percent could figure out how much medicine to give a child based on a chart of age and weight. Only 18 percent could locate a correct departure time on a bus schedule, and only 37 percent could figure out the correct change from $3 after buying two items from a lunch menu.[18]

Oregon governor, Barbara Roberts, captured the dilemma when she commented on the results: "How can an unemployed woman get to a job interview on time if she can't read the bus schedule?"[19]

There are degrees of illiteracy, of course, and no standard of measurement. At one end of the spectrum are those applicants who cannot complete an employment form because they can't read it, or write. Evidence indicates, however, that there are millions of people already on the job who can read and write to some degree but who have difficulty with their work because their literacy skills are marginal.

Motorola discovered, for instance, that when they changed the colors of the boxes holding a number of supplies in their factories, confusion ensued.[20] Some workers who could not read the labels on the boxes were operating satisfactorily because they knew where parts were located according to box color.

In defining literacy, most employers would agree with the definition put forward by the National Assessment of Education Progress: "Using printed and written information to function in society, to achieve one's goals, and to develop one's knowledge and potential."[21]

This practical approach to identifying literacy allows employers and workers alike to share a common set of goals. Yet few businesses require applicants to demonstrate literacy ability, in some cases for fear of administering racially, or ethnically, unfair tests.

As the most thoroughly studied facet of the U.S. educational landscape, literacy stands alone as a challenging problem for the United States. With as many as 20 million Americans unable to upgrade their skills and their economic prospects, the nation confronts a large obstacle to continued economic progress.[22] It is clear that all segments of our society—private and public—must join forces to help these citizens.

Literacy, of course, is an indication of the quality of the nation's education system. It is apparent that a great many students leave school unable to read and to reason well enough to hold good jobs and to be trained for higher-paying jobs.

For example, in Los Angeles, Laura Sanchez, who owns a sausage factory, reported that a new piece of equipment that could increase the output of her workforce went unused for months because none of the workers could be taught to operate it. Her business was endangered, as were the jobs of the employees.[23] Dedicated to upgrading its current workforce rather than finding new, better-educated workers, Motorola discovered that about half of its 25,000 manufacturing employees in the United States had math and English skills below the seventh grade level.[24]

Illiteracy is the most virulent symptom of the education malaise that affects the United States. But there are others. By all measures, America's kindergarten-through-12th-grade education system is second rate when compared to other nations. In test after test of reading and computational skills administered on an international basis, U.S. students flunk. In tests conducted by the International Association for the Evaluation of Educational Achievement (IAEEA) between 1983 and 1986, U.S. students ranked low in math and science at ages 10 and 14, and last at age 17.[25]

In commenting on this education gap, the Commission on Workforce Quality and Labor Market Efficiency said:

> Even taking into account institutional and cultural differences, the consistent and significant underachievement of American students, relative to their counterparts in other countries, is of grave concern. U.S. students lag behind in science and mathematics at every grade level and at every stratum of ability and background. Compared with students in the developed countries of Western Europe and the Pacific rim, the average mathematics attainment of students in our

middle and secondary schools places them in the bottom quartile. Worse perhaps, the top five percent of college-bound high-school seniors in the U.S. have scores in advanced mathematics comparable to the average score of all Japanese seniors.[26]

Other indicators are also discouraging. U.S. high school students spend about 3.5 hours per week on homework and 24 hours each week watching television. U.S. students attend school only about 180 days each year, compared to about 225 in the former West Germany, and 240 days in Japan.

These disheartening statistics continue to worsen despite the large, national effort underway since the landmark report by the U.S. Education Department in 1983. *A Nation at Risk* took the measure of America's education system and struck a responsive chord throughout the country. One comment in the report was particularly provocative:

> Secondary school curricula have been diffused to the point that they no longer have a central purpose. In effect, we have a cafeteria-style curriculum in which the appetizers and the desserts can easily be mistaken for the main courses. . . . This curricular smorgasboard, combined with extensive student choice, explains a great deal about where we find ourselves today.[27]

In his landmark study, *The Neglected Majority*, Dale Parnell also noted the failure of secondary schools in the United States to prepare noncollege-bound students for life. He pointed out that 36 percent of high school students were in an academic curriculum aimed at college while 42 percent were in a so-called general track and 19 percent in a vocational track.[28]

Interestingly, most high school dropouts are from the general curriculum—63 percent.[29] Only 6 percent of students in an academic track drop out and 29 percent from the vocational track.[30] Closer examination, however, provides some insight into this phenomenon.

General curriculum students attend classes in what Parnell calls "potluck in the school house," rather than the smorgasbord described in *A Nation at Risk*.[31] A mixture of general, remedial, and hobby courses comprise the typical general curriculum, with an emphasis on physical education, arts, crafts, and home economics courses. Whereas academic and vocational curriculum students have some ostensible purpose for attending high school, general curriculum students appear to be occupying time and space with little focus on either.

This enormous waste of human potential tells only part of the story. Because our education system is geared for the collegebound, 50 percent of our students do not receive career guidance and skill training.[32] In 1990, that meant that many of the 1.3 million students in a general curriculum were wasting their time in school. Additionally, dropouts—who number 800,000 annually—are learning the hard realities of trying to find meaningful work without a skill.[33]

Since *A Nation at Risk* appeared, 45 states have toughened graduation requirements and teacher certification standards. Teacher salaries have increased 18 percent in real terms during the period, and expenditures per pupil in the United States have increased 28 percent in real terms during the past decade.[34] The United States now spends more money per pupil than nearly all other countries in the world. It appears, however, that these steps have not had much effect. Test scores continue to drop and the dropout rate is unchanged.

Although U.S. students fare poorly on international academic tests, there is no evidence that they are less intelligent than others. In fact, there is considerable evidence that Americans can work equally as effectively as others, and in some cases more effectively. For instance, highly trained U.S. service personnel in the Gulf War operated sophisticated weapons systems in combat conditions without supervision. In addition, companies in the United States that have trained workers to operate as teams and then organized the workplace to take advantage of worker competency have equaled and sometimes surpassed productivity rates of foreign producers. The U.S. college system remains the best in the world, and the brightest students from other countries are flooding U.S. campuses for advanced learning.

For most of the 1980s, business joined with the education community in many states to help improve the education system. Some 140,000 business-school partnerships have been counted by the National Center for Educational Statistics.[35] Unfortunately, these activities did not change the way teachers teach and schools educate. They have been called "feel-good" projects because the businesses involved felt good about the projects but they did not focus on results, and they did not create the systemic changes needed in the system.

The U.S. education system does not just need a few more computers, a few mentors, and a few guest lecturers—it needs a total restructuring. This restructuring must include new governance, new teaching techniques, more decentralized decision making, and an approach to students that recognizes their varying learning styles and the important role each can play in the United States.

The evidence of the inadequacy of these business-education partnerships is contained in the data collected by the National Assessment of Education Progress (NAEP), a congressionally funded organization administered by the Educational Testing Service (ETS). Despite increases in spending, a great deal of attention and the involvement of business during the 1980s, NAEP came to the following conclusions:

1. There were no gains in reading ability during the decade.[36]
2. On average, there was some advancement in mathematics ability in the nation's schools but not at the high school level.[37]
3. There was some improvement in science ability at all age groups, but U.S. students remain in last place when compared to other industrialized nations.[38]
4. There was some improvement in writing ability among students, but the absolute levels of achievement remain poor.[39]

The case for a relative decline in the education quality of U.S. schools has been made: common tests of academic knowledge administered internationally show that our students do poorly in comparison with students from other industrialized nations.

The U.S. job market does not require that all new employees come to work already trained, but it is having difficulty assimilating high school dropouts and high school graduates who are unable to translate their schooling into usable job skills.

FIGURE 4–1
Estimated U.S. Power Consumption by Source

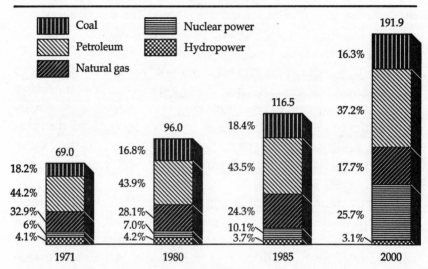

In the year 2000, which energy source is predicted to supply less power than coal?

A. Petroleum   C. Nuclear power   E. I don't know
B. Natural gas   D. Hydropower

Source: *From School to Work,* a Policy Information Report. Princeton, NJ: Policy Information Center, Educational Testing Service, 1990.

U.S. employers cannot afford to hire workers who cannot perform adequately and cannot afford to pay high wages to employees who can't handle knowledge work. In growing numbers, U.S. jobs are being lost to foreign workers who will work for less money or who are knowledgeable enough to function in new work environments that require fewer workers.

In testing conducted by NAEP, the gap between school learning and job proficiency has been graphically portrayed. Following are examples of the results of testing among high school students who ranked in the top 40 percent in reading ability.

Only 50 percent could determine the correct answer from Figure 4–1.[40] Only 83 percent could find a specific intersection on a city street map.[41] Only 30 percent could answer the questions related to the menu in Figure 4–2.[42]

And these results were obtained from the top 40 percent of high school readers! Clearly, we need to improve the correlation

FIGURE 4–2

A task typical of performance requires the reader to examine a menu to compute the cost of a specified meal and to determine the correct change from a specified amount. The difficulty of such tasks reflects the need to match information and then to apply two operations in sequence.

Suppose you had $3 to spend for lunch.

If you order a Lancaster Special sandwich and onion soup, how much change would you get back? _____
How much should you leave for a 10% tip? _____

Soups—Made by our Chef Daily

Onion soup	.60
Soup of the day	.60
Vichyssoise in summer	
Beef burgers, broiled to order;	1.85
1/4 lb. of the finest beef available, seasoned to perfection and served on a buttered bun	
Wine cheddar-cheese burger	1.95
Blue-cheese burger	1.95
Pineapple burger	1.95
Bacon burger	2.10
Wine cheddar-cheese and Bacon burger	2.25

Sandwiches

Sliced turkey—garnished	1.30
Turkey salad—garnished	.95
Chicken salad—garnished	.95
Tuna Fish salad—garnished	.95
Sliced beef tongue—garnished	1.50
Grilled wine cheddar-cheese	1.95
The Lancaster Special	1.95
Corned beef, melted Swiss cheese,	
Sauerkraut on seeded rye . . . Need we say more?	
Minimum check at lunch	1.00

Source: *From School to Work,* a Policy Information Report. Princeton, NJ: Policy Information Center, Educational Testing Service, 1990.

between high school learning and the requirements of work. The ability to use simple documents on the job is a common work requirement, but many employers have had to figure out how to structure work so that workers don't have to read.

Comparing these test results to the activity of workers who are operating in decentralized work environments provides insight into the reason U.S. businesses have been slow to join the high-performance work revolution.

FIGURE 4–3
Document Proficiency of High School Graduates without Postsecondary Degrees, 1986

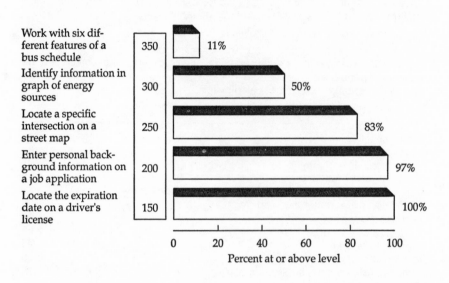

Source: *Profiles of Young Adult Literacy.* Irwin Kirsch and Ann Jungeblut, National Assessment of Educational Progress, Educational Testing Service, 1986.

Here is additional insight into what our students don't know and can't accomplish:

- Over one third of 11th graders in the United States cannot adequately write a description of a summer job they would like to have and their qualifications for having it.[43]
- 14 percent of all students assessed by NAEP don't know which part of a light bulb glows.[44]
- 92 percent of our students cannot select the object with greatest density when given specified mass and volume for several objects.[45]

In the United States, about 13 percent of our students quit school permanently when they are 16 or 17, with the remainder receiving either their regular high school diplomas or an equivalent degree, such as the General Equivalency Diploma.[46] About half of those who graduate at age 18 are enrolled in two-year or four-year colleges the following October.[47] These statistics are about the same for white and black students, but a greater percentage of Hispanic students drop out of high school.[48]

Much has been made of how poorly college-bound U.S. high school graduates perform on international tests compared to students from other nations, but little has been written about the fate of those teenagers who do not care to go to college, or even complete high school. Like it or not, nearly one third of the jobs in the United States don't require a full 12 years of schooling.[49] Although we might hope that the size of this group would decline, we should also recognize the valuable role it could play in the U.S. economy if the individuals in this group were better educated and if their skills were upgraded.

These American workers, although at the bottom of the economic ladder, could play a much more valuable role for employers if they were better educated. The employers of this group will keep a lid on wages and standards of living if they do not receive better-qualified workers who can make a larger contribution to profits.

The ramifications of a noncompetitive education system for U.S. business are quite severe. Some companies that depend on low-skill, low-wage workers may maintain their profitability in the short run as they supply the U.S. underclass with relatively low-cost, low-quality goods. However, as international businesses increasingly establish manufacturing and service sources in emerging countries, it is unlikely that U.S. wages will be competitive even at the low end. Foreign producers will figure out how to produce some of these less expensive goods by employing smarter but fewer workers and then displace U.S. jobs through imports.

In addition to a growing dependence on low-wage workers, another educational fact of life that the United States has sidestepped is the issue of school dropouts. In one sense, taxpayers have a stake in the failure of these students. Taxes are levied to pay only for educating students who attend school—that is, every student who drops out reduces the tax burden. States compile education budgets based on projections of how many students will be in school, not on the basis of how many children

need to be educated. Thus, projections for dropouts are included and the final education bill as computed in this manner is
the basis for tax planning in every state. The national average for
education expenditures per pupil is $4,600.[50] With 800,000 stu-
dents dropping out of school each year, taxpayers are saving
$3.7 billion each year.[51]

On a macro basis, the price we are paying for allowing dropouts to remain undereducated, undertrained, and underem-
ployed far exceeds the investment it would take to upgrade their
abilities. It is estimated by the Committee for Economic Development (CED) that each year's class of dropouts costs the nation
over $240 billion of lost incomes and taxes over the lifetimes of the
students.[52] CED also estimates that it costs society an additional
$10 billion in taxpayer funds to pay for crime, drug, prison, and
welfare expenses associated with each class of dropouts.[53]

As Derek Bok, the former president of Harvard University,
said, "If you think education is expensive, try ignorance."

But, when it comes to taxes, the public remains focused on
the short term. Is it any wonder that the compulsory age for education continues to stop at 16? To raise it would require higher
taxes. Still another tail wagging the dog is the 9-month, 180-day
school year in the United States—the vestige of a 19th-century
agrarian economy that depended on its youth to work the fields
in the summer. The tax bill for another month of school currently
appears to be politically untenable.

There is plenty of evidence that these expedient views are
destructive. Studies conducted by Baumol, Blackman, and
Wolff, and reported in *Productivity and American Leadership*, demonstrate how education improves the productivity and the standard of living of a nation.[54] That is, the education of an individual
not only helps that person achieve a better standard of living but
also makes an additional contribution to the society's standard.

The study also reports other interesting information that indicates the need for improving the U.S. education system. For
example, Figure 4–4 illustrates the progress that lesser-
developed nations have made in educating their populations.[55]
By 1984, there was little difference between all nations in the
number of people who attended grade school. A gap remained

FIGURE 4–4
International comparisons of educational attendance (primary, second-
ary, and higher), percent of age group enrolled. 1965 and 1984. (For some
countries with universal primary education, the gross enrollment ratios
may exceed or fall below 100% because some pupils are above or below
the country's standard primary-school age.)

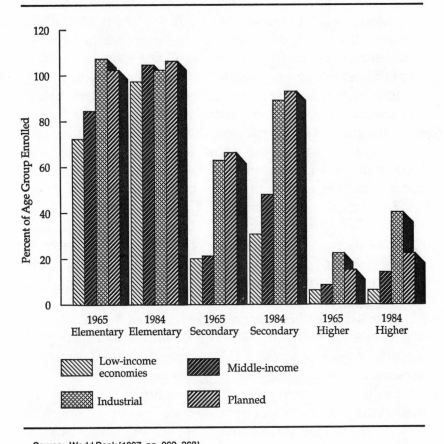

Source: World Bank [1987, pp. 262–263].

between underdeveloped and developed nations for secondary
school attendance, but it had narrowed.

This trend indicates that these countries will eventually assume greater importance in world commerce, that still another
wave of educated, low-paid people looms just over the horizon
to replace the Koreans and other emerging nationals as formidable sources of workers.

Still another inference drawn from this study is the need to upgrade the education of minority people in the United States. Comparing the U.S. minority bloc to a lesser-developed nation, the study demonstrates the dilutive effect undereducated people will have on the nation's productivity in the years ahead.

According to the U.S. Office of Technology Assessment, in 1988, black and Hispanic people constituted 23.6 percent of the nation's laborforce aged 16–24.[56] The rate of growth of these minority groups implies that by the year 2000, they will constitute nearly 30 percent of the workforce in the United States.[57]

Studies indicate a direct link between educational attainment and national productivity, and demographic data indicate that minority groups are a growing force within the American workforce.[58] This adds up to a requirement that the American underclass be brought into the mainstream of American life for national economic reasons in addition to reasons of democratic values.

Economically and socially, the United States cannot afford to allow this growing subclass of low-paid, low-skilled, low-contributing segment of society to continue growing in numbers. The frustrations of class distinctions will manifest themselves in some form eventually but probably after it is too late to cure the problem.

Business must become an active advocate for change that will reverse this situation, rather than continue as a silent partner with an education system that ensures that a third of our citizens remain mired in the mud of ignorance.

Business has an economic self-interest in upgrading the skills of dropouts and other undereducated youth. According to a study by The Hudson Institute, there will be enough jobs created in America by the next century to maintain full employment in the United States.[59] Although there will always be a certain amount of unemployment, as the overall labor pool shrinks relative to the number of jobs, there will be upward pressure on wages in this country. Combined with continuing inroads of foreign competitors in the U.S. market, U.S. businesses will find profitability squeezed. It makes sense to upgrade the skills of this large cohort of undereducated workers—and their wages—so they can work in more efficient work environments.

Another reason business must become an advocate for education improvement is that the public in general is not aware of the linkage between education and a nation's standard of living. Also, the public does not know that many U.S. workers now compete for their jobs on an international scale.

U.S. business cannot continue to compete internationally or expect to improve profitability with a poorly educated workforce. Unfortunately, part of the problem is the attitude of average Americans regarding the education problem.

Only 38 percent of American families have children under the age of 18, which calls into question how interested the majority is in the problem of education (particularly if there is a tax increase associated with the solution).[60]

In a survey taken by Phi Delta Kappa, about 80 percent of Americans said they were aware that there is a serious national education problem; but 70 percent said that their children's schools are doing fine, which means that there is little grassroots support for change to the education system (if education improvement is the product, the customer isn't buying).[61]

According to a national poll conducted by the Gallup Organization, three quarters of Americans believe that the problem of U.S. competitiveness is that the work ethic is stronger in other nations than here. These people do not believe there is a need to improve the education system as a way to improve business competitiveness.[62]

In a series of focus-group interviews conducted by the Public Agenda Foundation for the Business-Higher Education Forum in 1990, a malaise was uncovered that does not bode well for developing a national consensus on education improvement.[63] The Foundation discovered a panoply of excuses for not restructuring education. A number of reasons were offered for declining U.S. business competitiveness other than undertrained and undereducated workers. People believe international trade problems are caused by foreign aid, by a lack of patriotism when people buy foreign goods, by corporate greed, by labor unions, and by foreign investment in the United States.[64]

The public believes workforce problems are work-ethic problems, not training problems. Finally, many Americans believe that if a true crisis develops, the United States will simply pull itself together and fix it. World War II, the space program, the Gulf War, and other emergencies the nation has overcome lead this group to rationalize that we can relax until it's time to make a comeback—a "hail Mary" football play for the education system.

The business community in the United States—small and large businesses—must lead the effort to overcome these attitudes and then lead the effort to restore our education system to first-class status. The fact is, you now need to be as well educated to go to work as to college. The education gap between the United States and other countries must be closed, and the business community is the only sector of the economy with the experience and the leadership to help educators make the massive changes necessary.

PART 2

CLOSING THE COMPETITIVE GAP

CHAPTER 5

OVERVIEW

Throughout the history of the United States, its economy has developed at a competitive pace and has raised the standard of living for its citizens. After trailing developed nations of the 18th and 19th centuries, the United States burst into the lead in the 20th century and has created an environment for most of its residents that is the envy of most of the world.

But, things are changing and the U.S. economic advance has slowed. In the long term, this reduction in the growth of economic slowdown will have profound effects. We are creating an untenable schism between large numbers of rich and poor people. We are losing our independence as other nations invade our markets and finance our debts. Eventually, the United States may become the third richest market, following Japan and a unified Europe.

Whether economists in the 21st century rank the United States first or second in productivity and whether citizens enjoy the world's highest standard of living 50 years from now is less important than reversing the destructive trends that have developed in the past quarter century. Productivity growth must be accelerated, the wealth gap must be closed by raising the incomes of the bottom third of the population, and U.S. businesses must improve their competitiveness.

In one sense, the very characteristics that created the U.S. economic miracle are now working against the nation's ability to compete with businesses in other countries. Historical distrust of government allowed business to operate mostly unfettered for a century and, although many would argue that government has become an intrusive force in the economy, the fact is the United States remains a free-market nation.

This contrasts with the experience of the business community in many other countries in which business is in partnership with government to achieve mutually agreeable goals. In many cases, business establishes the goals and government focuses resources on them.

It's fair to say, however, that the United States has the government and the economic policies its citizens desire. Regardless of which political party is in control of the federal levers of power or in each of the states, America's economic, business, and workforce systems reflect the American will. Attitudes wander a meandering course swinging from left to right and then back again, but at any given moment government policies generally are congruent with public priorities.

Unfortunately, the U.S. system of government appears to have evolved in a way that encourages its political leaders to follow rather than lead public opinion on domestic matters. From time to time, a courageous leader will take the unpopular path, but does so at his or her peril if things don't turn out right. For this reason, U.S. political leaders at the federal level have focused more on foreign relations than on domestic matters for the past several decades—the voting public appears to have turned that part of the government over to them.

This historical tradition of noninterference by government, combined with generous amounts of public ennui regarding economics and business problems, has created a vacuum in a number of institutions that the public expects the experts to address. Improving the education system surely must be a complex and arcane task best undertaken by educational professionals; skills training and school-to-work transitions are complex public/private sector activities; employee training is, by definition, something that employers, not the public or the government, should address. The United States must develop an *attitude* toward work and workers before business can improve the quality of the U.S. workforce. It's up to business in the United States to build this attitude.

The challenge of engaging the public in this activity is daunting. Large blocs of the public are apparently satisfied with the economic status quo or don't understand the linkages between business productivity, worker skills, and economic improvement.

- Even as the U.S. population is aging, older people have gained economically faster than other segments of the population and don't believe they have a stake in the quality of education or the quality of the workforce.
- The best educated in the nation—about 25 percent of the population—have increased their wealth considerably during the past 10 years and generally are not aware of economic problems.[1]
- Wage earners who have seen their buying power actually decline during the past decade have sent their wives and their teenagers into the job market and then borrowed to the hilt, thus avoiding an unacceptable decline in their standard of living.
- Despite repeated warnings about the declining quality of education, there is little agitation at the local level for meaningful change because nearly 80 percent of the households in the United States don't have children in school.[2]

Accordingly, an important task for U.S. business is to generate attention to these problems and then explain the importance of new public policies in resolving them. The nation's historical antipathy for business/government partnerships must be overcome so that political leaders are able to help without fear of voter reprisal. Although political parties may disagree on the tactics to use in the battle to upgrade the United States, they must agree that the United States has a problem.

In his landmark essay, *The Structure of Scientific Revolutions*, Thomas S. Kuhn described the process the scientific community undergoes to advance understanding of scientific matters. The essay has become a roadmap for all those who wish to change an established method of operating or of thinking because its basic principles explain how transformations occur throughout society, not just in science.[3]

Kuhn proposes that experts won't alter the way they think

and act until they have a more attractive alternative model to follow. Using the history of science and scientific evolution as examples, he demonstrates that scientists will continue to advance understanding of old paradigms even when data and observations run contrary to accepted beliefs. When, however, a new paradigm is proposed—one that appears to resolve the anomalies between observed nature and the old paradigm—scientists adopt the new and proceed eagerly and energetically to prove its worth.

In this usage, paradigms are not perfection. They are new proposals that have the force of logic and sensibility. New para-' digms allow experts to experiment and make contributions to their chosen fields. They leave room for advancing knowledge and personal accomplishment. Because they do, knowledge advances at a rapid rate in the period after a new paradigm is proposed and accepted.

The United States needs several new paradigms:

- For administering schools and for teaching
- For training youths who do not graduate from college
- For training workers and for organizing work
- For organizing economic development resources in every American community

Interestingly, just as scientific experiments and observations of nature have always provided anomalies that don't fit the current paradigm, the United States has confronted anomalies that challenge the way we educate and train workers and organize work. For example, students in other nations score better on tests than U.S. students, but we cling to the old educational paradigm.[4] Other nations produce highly skilled workers who can handle new technologies, but we continue to disregard the needs of 75 percent of our youths who never finish college.[5] Companies in other nations realize greater efficiency through modern work environments, but we continue to implement the old paradigm—the Tayloristic mass-production system invented nearly 100 years ago.

The role of business, then, is to push for establishment of

new paradigms that experts can refine and improve upon. Among these should be a change in the education system in the United States. Business should help pioneering educators and political leaders create better schools so that the rest of the education community can leave the old paradigm and enjoy the experience of expanding and refining the new paradigm.

Business must galvanize public opinion in favor of a reorganization of existing systems that were created to help people work so that labor-market experts can apply their experience to a more productive paradigm.

Business must reorganize itself so that managers can experience the joy of real decision making, and frontline workers can realize their true potential.

It's not clear, however, that business people comprehend the basic shift that has occurred in markets during the past 10 to 15 years, and until they do, they won't understand why they must upgrade their workforces and they won't understand what the end game is for their businesses.

The fundamental change that has occurred in business is a shift from mass-produced, standardized delivery of products and services to a mass-produced, customized delivery of products and services. To the extent this delivery is taking place on a global basis, businesses and workforces are competing in a wider arena.

Mass production in this definition refers to services as well as factory production; it is the traditional achievement of volume business as a method for reducing unit costs. Customized delivery refers to the perception of the customer that he or she has as much choice as possible regarding product specifications, which might include speed of delivery.

The implications of customized delivery are profound and defy old-fashioned business intuitions developed through Tayloristic teaching and experiences. The Tayloristic concept divided products into two categories—commodities, which were produced in very high volumes in order to achieve low unit cost, and value-added products, which were usually custom designed. The world of business can no longer be divided in this manner.

Price-sensitive commodity products remain, but the market niches for value-added versions of them continue to grow. New technologies and new work organizations allow short runs at low unit costs. Moreover, it is now possible to achieve the advantages of mass production without utilizing large numbers of assembly-line workers.

It's possible, for instance, to upgrade the ability of a workforce and reorganize the workplace in a manner to increase productivity substantially. Then, the decision is whether to pass along the improved profitability to customers in the form of lower prices as a way to increase market share. In some cases, a marketing advantage can be gained by reorganizing delivery systems or by expert manipulation of inventories in order to become a reliable source of supply regardless of current economic conditions. Companies that interface with the public at the retail level can provide extraordinary customer service through the combination of a well-trained set of customer representatives and a well-designed computer system—the entire catalog industry has been established on this concept.

Overlaying all these changes is a byproduct of more efficient production that many customers now take for granted—top-notch quality. Although it is still possible to price versions of many products according to their quality, growing numbers of customers demand that the least expensive versions be more reliable than in the past. Quality is not an option offered; it is an aspect assumed.

The U.S. textile industry provides an interesting example of the problems confronted by U.S. management as it tackles these chores. For some time, the American textile industry has competed with foreign products produced on advanced equipment by low-wage workers.[6] This problem was compounded by a wave of new technology and rapidly changing styles that virtually made obsolete the concept of long production runs of a few designs.[7]

An early response to this foreign threat was to move mills to the South, where wage rates were low.[8] Combined with investment in a new generation of textile production equipment, this shift advanced productivity faster than the U.S. manufacturing average during the 1970s and 1980s.[9] But, imports continued to flow into the U.S.—inexpensive fabrics from low-wage countries and upscale fabrics from high-wage countries with up-to-date equipment.[10]

The industry responded intelligently by discovering niches within the U.S. market it could serve rapidly and competitively.[11] Textile companies began offering greater variety, with mills increasing their style offerings by up to 1,000 percent.[12] New computer-controlled equipment allows mills to make low, efficient runs using many of the features now found in a modern work organization.[13]

Concurrently, mill managers reordered the way workers operated in the production environment.[14] After little change for decades, work in textile mills changed dramatically during the 1980s.[15] Textile mill machines now require computer-literate operators, not manual operators whose best skills were to tie broken threads quickly. Reading computer outputs and entering new machine instructions, diagnosing machine stoppages and then entering repair codes all require reading, analysis, and keyboard skills in an environment that a few years ago didn't even require a literate workforce.[16]

Although the industry has reorganized the workplace, it is struggling with the problem of finding a qualified workforce. It now hires people with two-year technical associate degrees in jobs it used to fill with workers who never finished high school.[17] Because of the industry's history, most young people in the semi-rural areas where its mills are located seek to escape traditional employment in the mills.[18]

The industry is coping with focused training of present employees and cooperative programs with community colleges and other consortia.[19] Literacy programs have been established in many locations.[20] But, the jury is out on whether the textile industry's workforce can be made congruent with the technology and work systems already installed in its mills. The industry faces the dilemma more and more U.S. industries will confront in the years ahead, and the outcome will be determined by its ability to upgrade the skills of its people.

Each of the old paradigms in the United States that must be

abandoned—education, training, and organization—is complex and each has powerful proponents, a fact that can frustrate a business person who wishes to make a difference. In many companies, it saps the energy of the leadership just to implement straightforward changes in decision making and organization. Many business people have been frustrated by the intransigence of school officials to recognize the need for improvement in their schools. Changing the entire governmental system for handling displaced, undertrained, and disadvantaged workers appears to be an impossible task.

The good news is that a great deal of work has already been accomplished in designing these new paradigms. There has not been enough cohesion, so the experts have not yet abandoned the old models and gravitated fully to the new, but there are encouraging indications that they are prepared to adopt new approaches—if they can participate and if they are not victimized by the change.

From a competitive standpoint, U.S. business has the opportunity to leapfrog competitors in other nations with new systems that combine the best elements of the American culture with the best elements of models already in use in other countries.

For example, businesses in countries, such as Germany, that have close relationships with the government have surrendered a fair amount of freedom and flexibility in exchange. In return for a national business focus, these societies require that business accept a very strong social contract with workers. Thus, companies in these countries may not have the right to reduce staffs when demand drops, and in some cases don't have the right to operate factories on weekends.

In some countries, such as Singapore, the government has a focused view of workforce training and mandates certain activity through taxes and other mechanisms that reduce profits.[21]

The fact that businesses in these nations continue to be successful despite these impediments is testimony to the powerful nature of worker education, training, and empowerment. The potential advantage U.S. business has is to realize a workforce of equal quality and to operate in the less-restrictive environment offered in this country. Moreover, like the scientists who refine a new paradigm in physics, biology, or genetics, U.S. businesses can refine the paradigms already in place in other nations and gain additional knowledge and insight.

Before these changes can be achieved, business leaders must accept the concept that the quality of the U.S. workforce is not a factor of remote systems over which business has no influence or control. Business people in the United States must view the entire U.S. workforce as an asset that is just as important as factories, technology, and cash. Although many companies have long proclaimed in annual reports that "people are our most important asset," at best, the chief executive officers had in mind the professional staffs. Frontline workers must now be viewed as critical components of corporate strategy.

Once this attitude is adopted, business people will realize the need to assume far greater responsibility for the U.S. education system, its school-to-work systems, and for employee training. The United States must create a pool of top-flight workers from which businesses can draw. The mobile nature of our people requires that a high school diploma from North Carolina be as meaningful as a high school diploma from Massachusetts. If a corporation trains workers and then has to lay them off for some reason, other companies should be eager to hire them, just as the original company should be eager to draw from the pool when its problems are resolved. High school dropouts and disadvantaged people must be upgraded, not just because U.S. businesses will need them to fill new jobs created in the 1990s, but because eventually society will not tolerate a large group of poor people in this country. Ignorance and indifference will eventually destroy a democracy.

Thus, business must help convince the public and elected officials that all Americans have a stake in improving these systems, and then convince the same groups that the time has come for these systems to orient themselves more toward the needs of business. It's time for the nation to achieve a consensus regarding workforce quality.

For example, workers whose children have grown and left home may believe that they no longer have a stake in the quality of the U.S. education system. Perhaps they would be more concerned if they knew that when they retire 20 years from now, the baby-boom generation will swell the ranks of social security recipients and that the number of workers in the workforce will decline. For about 25 years after 2010, the number of retirees per 100 workers will rise steadily.[22] Those workers must be highly paid if they are to pay the increased burden imposed by the social security system. Moreover, if today's employees expect a good pension from their employer, they should hope their companies can compete profitably in worldwide markets. This profitability requires a qualified workforce.

The fact of the matter is, everyone in the United States has a stake in the success of U.S. businesses, and the public knows intuitively that the nation's standard of living is connected directly to business performance. What too few people understand are the linkages between education, worker skills, workforce organization, international competition, and business success. Unfortunately, too few business people understand the same issues, and too many who do have a short-term attitude toward their enterprise.

It's vital that business gains a greater degree of trust by Americans so that government-business cooperative systems can be established that allow business to have a louder voice in the use of tax dollars for education and training. In every U.S. community, a new system must be built that combines existing government and business resources and then focuses them on economic development, including upgrading of worker skills and the restructuring of our schools.

In Germany, for instance, regional chambers of employers are legally designated as the agencies responsible for administering apprenticeship programs and other in-company training leading to certification of workers.[23] This seamless interface of public and private-sector programs and funding reflects a consensus in that country that training is vital and that business has the expertise to deliver it.

Large companies in Germany operate their own vocational schools. Apprentices attend a company-operated school each morning. In the afternoon, they work in the factory and laboratories. Teachers also work in the factory so they can keep their vocational expertise current.

The strategies required to improve the nation's education system and the other mechanisms that affect the quality of the workforce are business strategies. Although business won't invent the new education paradigm, it must lead the call for change and help those educators who agree. The same approach applies to school-to-work training systems and to workplace training. Businesses at all levels must go to work to tilt the bulk of public opinion toward these new paradigms. If they are not adopted, business in this country will not succeed in operating within the new international competition paradigm.

CHAPTER 6

CLOSING THE ORGANIZATION GAP

The organization of all work in the United States during the 20th century has approximated the Tayloristic model of functional and hierarchical division: specialists, both white-collar and blue-collar, are employed to perform specific tasks that require specific training; decisions are made at ascending layers of supervision, depending on importance.

This smoothly operating system served business well for decades and led to workforce roles that were fairly well defined early in life for a large percentage of the workforce. A small cadre of middle- and upper-level people went to college and became the managers and executives who managed U.S. business. As late as the 1950s, only 60 percent of the nation's youths graduated from high school.[1]

The landscape of U.S. business has changed dramatically during the past 25 years, but too many of the businesses comprising that landscape have clung to old models of operating. The service sector now accounts for 70 percent of the U.S. economy.[2] Technology—computers, video, robots, satellites, sensors—has revolutionized products and production. Businesses now operate on a global basis, and the United States has many competitors now compared to just a few decades ago.

Despite this dramatic shift in business dynamics, U.S. management continues to organize along the lines of mass-production manufacturing models rather than to design customized work organizations. Interestingly, evidence indicates that manufacturing management is changing the way work is organized faster than service-sector managers.

There is little question that many businesses have not modernized their organizations because their employees are not capable of operating in a decentralized environment. To the extent that the education system did not advance the level of learning of noncollege-bound students in the past 20 years, business did not advance the way work was done.

Although high school graduation rates and college enrollment rates climbed steadily during the post–World War II period, many students did not leave high school with the skills necessary for assuming greater responsibilities. With its principal focus on college-bound students, U.S. high schools failed to educate the others at world-class levels. For the first time in our history, a generation of students were not expected to know more than their parents.

Despite this lack of educational advancement, for some years there was a rough balance between the quality of education, the size of the workforce, and the worker needs of business in the United States. In other countries, however, new forms of work organization were being developed that exploited an organized approach to developing worker skills.

Germany, for example, focused on high-quality niches for manufactured products and on high technology products in its large chemical industry, both of which built on the value-added ability of its highly trained work force. Japan having decided that the intellect of its work force was its only possibility for achieving comparative advantage, established a culture that produces a high school graduation rate of over 90 percent.[3]

Concurrently, the government/business systems evolving in these countries smoothed the transition from school to work and reflected a national will to educate and train everyone. Both blue-collar work and white-collar work in these countries are considered equally important to the national economies.

During the past decade, U.S. business has begun to recognize the power of these new work systems and has begun to experiment with a U.S. version. The total quality movement, although not an organizational concept, was the embryo for these experiments. During the 1970s, Philip Crosby began describing the economic advantages of eliminating scrap, rework, quality-control departments, and similar inefficiencies in the manufacturing plant by instilling in employees the need to "do it right the first time." Management discovered that a five-step process that was 96 percent perfect at each step resulted in a final rate of acceptance of only 82 percent.

This was the beginning of expanding worker empowerment because it required management to explain the context of each worker's job; it required dialogue. This version of quality improvement was based on simple profit improvement logic and was not customer-oriented. For that reason, not many companies bothered to install quality systems 15 or 20 years ago because U.S. business continued to dominate U.S. markets and was not threatened by high-quality products from overseas. The consumer was used to a product that was only 82 percent "perfect."

In Japan, the legendary W. Edwards Deming taught factory management how to install Statistical Process Control, which required workers to monitor production and to maintain prescribed tolerances. Although this system was not organizationally oriented, it began to affect the way work was organized. It was not a large step for Japanese managers to insist that parts bought from vendors be perfect and then to insist that they be delivered as needed rather than stored as inventory. After all, if all the parts are perfect, there is no need to keep spares around to replace the defective parts. This was the just-in-time (JIT) system. With this intense focus on quality, it was natural to form quality circles where employees could exchange ideas and then to begin communicating with designers and engineers regarding improvements. This continuous improvement process is called kaizen.

For a long time, Americans believed that these superior products were competing with U.S.-produced goods at competitive prices because workers in these countries were paid low wages and "buy American" became fashionable. Over time, however, the differences in performance became too wide to ignore simply for patriotic reasons. As products from Europe and Japan became more available in the United States, quality became a marketing lever.

The desire to improve the quality of products does not normally begin with a discussion of work organization, but the ability of a company to achieve high rates of quality inevitably leads to changes in the way work is accomplished. Happily, companies that have focused on quality improvement have also reduced costs, usually at three levels—less expense for scrap and rework, less expense for supervisors and specialists, and greater productivity per worker. In turn, this has caused change in work organization.

This discussion begins at the other end. That is, quality improvement should be one of the outcomes of a well-organized work environment. That has been the German experience. German businesses do not have nearly the intensity of Japanese businesses regarding quality; good quality is a natural outgrowth of a system in Germany that begins with proud craftsmen who are so highly paid that the only business strategy that makes sense is to focus on niches in markets that are willing to pay high prices for superior products. By the same token, German workers are organized in a fashion that produces more unit output per person than in traditional work systems.

This discussion also departs at a point that assumes that workers have the education and training to work in these new organizations. It is senseless to empower workers who are unprepared.

Business strategies for closing the work-organization gap are mostly internal to each business. There are a few public-policy possibilities that business can utilize—such as the assistance of local labor-market systems, which will be discussed in the final chapter. New work organizations are the environments in which better-educated and better-trained employees are able to be more productive, so federal, state, and local government can be of most help to business in helping to upgrade the workforce.

Any discussion of business organization must be somewhat general because business needs and capabilities vary considerably by industry, size, profitability, and other factors. Moreover, the characteristics of manufacturing businesses are significantly different than service businesses, and there is a wide range of profiles within the service sector. However, a number of systems fairly common to all businesses must be overlayed on new forms of work organization.

Finally, the most pervasive concept available to management as we near the 21st century, one that undergirds all discussion of work organization, is the availability of information, usually through computers. Computers allow modern management to decentralize and to empower employees at lower levels while gaining *more* control and *more* information related to the business. By empowering employees to record their work on interconnected computer systems, management gains instant access to the status of the work. Interrelated computer systems can then determine optimum levels of inventory and shipping schedules. Far-flung field sales forces have quicker access to information about availability of products and about the status of customer orders; and financial managers have current knowledge regarding uses of cash, revenues, and payables.

An example is the system that Wal-Mart department stores has installed to interface with most of its suppliers. As Wal-Mart employees sell products, cash registers capture information and forward it to a central data base that suppliers can view concurrently with Wal-Mart management. Thus, suppliers know every day how many of their products are sold, the status of Wal-Mart inventories, and when to ship new stocks. The result is a smooth manufacturing cycle and less inventory, which saves money for suppliers and Wal-Mart.[4]

Decentralization and worker authority empowers management every bit as much as it empowers frontline workers and, in the end, this change in work organization may be the most important facet of new work systems in many companies.

Although each business environment is different, the basic principles underpinning these new systems can be applied universally:

1. Greater management flexibility, including the ability to make changes recommended by workers.
2. On-going worker training, including remedial mathematics and reading when necessary.

3. Greater worker autonomy, including greater responsibility for a broader range of tasks.
4. More communications between workers and management, including feedback on product design and production problems.
5. Less bureaucracy and paperwork, which implies greater utilization of computers to capture and interpret information.

Table 6-1 indicates a number of differences between old and new ways of organizing work.[5]

Manufacturing

(The following discussion of Dresser and Ford is based heavily on unpublished research conducted by the Commission on the Skills of the American Work Force.)

Generally, two types of new organizations in manufacturing companies have developed during the past 20 years or so—cellular manufacturing and team manufacturing. The desired effect of these approaches is a reduction of the number of indirect personnel in the manufacturing process, less work-in-process, less inventory, higher quality, and better productivity due to greater employee involvement.

Cellular manufacturing work systems incorporate a series of processes that combine to produce a component, part, or assembly. Normally, there are 5 to 10 machines in the series manned by two to five operators who handle the entire sequence of manufacturing steps. The workers move the component from machine to machine, perform their own inspection after each step, change their own tools, and perform simple repairs to their machines.

This approach to manufacturing reduces the number of people involved in the manufacturing process, and reduces work-in-process (WIP). It is a just-in-time (JIT) system in that parts and components move from one manufacturing cell to the next as

TABLE 6–1
Changing Organizational Patterns in U.S. Industry

Old model	New model
Mass production, *1950s and 1960s*	*Flexible decentralization,* *1980s and beyond*

Overall strategy

Old model	New model
• Low cost through vertical integration, mass production, scale economies, long production runs.	• Low cost with no sacrifice of quality, coupled with substantial flexibility, through partial vertical disintegration, greater reliance on purchased components and services.
• Centralized corporate planning; rigid managerial hierarchies.	• Decentralization of decision making; flatter hierarchies.
• International sales primarily through exporting and direct investment.	• Multimode international operations, including minority joint ventures and nonequity strategic alliances.

Product design and development

Old model	New model
• Internal and hierarchical; in the extreme, a linear pipeline from central corporate research laboratory to development to manufacturing engineering.	• Decentralized, with carefully managed division of responsibility among R&D and engineering groups; simultaneous product and process development where possible; greater reliance on suppliers and contract engineering firms.
• Breakthrough innovation the ideal goal.	• Incremental innovation and continuous improvement valued.

Production

Old model	New model
• Fixed or hard automation.	• Flexible automation.
• Cost control focuses on direct labor.	• With direct costs low, reductions of indirect cost become critical.
• Outside purchases based on arm's-length, price-based competition; many suppliers.	• Outside purchasing based on price, quality, delivery, technology; fewer suppliers.
• Off-line or end-of-line quality control.	• Real-time, on-line quality control.
• Fragmentation of individual tasks, each specified in detail; many job classifications.	• Selective use of work groups; multiskilling, job rotation; few job classifications.

TABLE 6–1 (concluded)

• Shop floor authority vested in first-line supervisors; sharp separation between labor and management.	• Delegation, within limits, of shop floor responsibility and authority to individuals and groups; blurring of boundaries between labor and management encouraged.

Hiring and human relations practices

• Workforce mostly full-time, semi-skilled. • Minimal qualifications acceptable. • Layoffs and turnover a primary source of flexibility; workers, in the extreme, viewed as a variable cost.	• Smaller core of full-time employees, supplemented with contingent (part-time, temporary, and contract) workers, who can be easily brought in or let go, as a major source of flexibility. • Careful screening of prospective employees for basic and social skills, and trainability. • Core workforce viewed as an investment, management attention to quality-of-working life as a means of reducing turnover.

Job ladders

• Internal labor market; advancement through the ranks via seniority and informal on-the-job training.	• Limited internal labor market; entry or advancement may depend on credentials earned outside the workplace.

Governing metaphors

• Supervisors as policemen, organization as army.	• Supervisors as coaches or trainers, organization as athletic team. (The Japanese metaphor; organization as family.)

Training

• Minimal for production workers, except for informal on-the-job training. • Specialized training (including apprenticeships) for grey-collar craft and technical workers.	• Short training sessions as needed for core workforce, sometimes motivational, sometimes intended to improve quality control practices or smooth the way for new technology. • Broader skills sought for both blue- and grey-color workers.

Source: Office of Technology Assessment, 1990.

they are completed, and there is no WIP inventory that cell operators draw from.

Dresser Industries adopted the cellular form of manufacturing in 1985 at its Houston facility. The Houston plant now produces high-quality hand-held power tools.

During the 1970s, heavy equipment was produced at this location, but the business began to lose market share to Asian companies that were underpricing Dresser. The decision was made to convert the facility to production of power tools in a specialty niche of the market that has characteristics such as low production runs, high quality, and high prices. Dresser strategized that its high-wage work force could only be used to produce high value-added products. The plant's customers include Boeing, GM, and BMW, which now orders 80 percent of its tools from the company.

As part of the conversion, in 1985 the plant began to install cellular manufacturing techniques, and by 1990, over half of the factory-floor operators were working in cells.

The two principal areas in the plant are machining and assembly. About 40 people work in the assembly area, with each worker assembling a complete tool. Each assembler must know how to assemble a number of tools and know how to read blueprints. Working in a private cubicle on the factory floor, an assembler must gather his bill of materials for each tool. He may build one tool or several at a time, depending on the status of work in progress. He signs a tag on each completed tool, and the tool is then forwarded to an inspection area where quality is checked.

Before Dresser established cellular operations, each worker in the machining area was responsible for one type of machining operation on one machine. Under the new system, each worker has mastered seven machining operations. Before restructuring the work, a product moved from one machining step to the next, resulting in batches of work-in-process and parts inventory at each station to ensure that work was not interrupted. Now, because the products move smoothly through the manufacturing process under the guidance of a single worker, there is much less WIP.

In the machining area, workers do their own quality inspection after completing each step of the process. Although there is a final inspection, quality-control (QC) checks after each step, performed by a centralized QC department, have been eliminated, reducing the amount of WIP.

Also, workers now have direct access to the tool room, which has been relocated to the factory floor. This has eliminated indirect workers from the process and speeded set-up time considerably.

Working in cooperation with its union, Dresser management negotiated a new job classification called "Production Center Technician," which requires a worker to master seven machines. Each worker is given two years to achieve this grade and then given a raise when he is certified. In 1989, the base rate for the machining area at this facility was $12.35 per hour, with the rate for Production Center Technicians set at $15.28—high value-added, high-wage.

The result of this strategic reorientation of the Dresser plant in Houston has been dramatic. For six consecutive years, costs at the plant dropped, and it exceeded internal return-on-investment targets.

The second type of nontraditional manufacturing work system is the team approach. In team manufacturing, salaried and wage employees work side-by-side to produce a component or an entire product, usually with total responsibility for decisions related to the manufacturing process. The system is characterized by universal responsibility for production rather than responsibility focused just in management, or salaried ranks. Frontline workers are immersed in the process and provided the opportunity to share their ideas and their expertise. The U.S. version of manufacturing teaming tends to follow a sports model, with a high degree of camaraderie and team pride.

Perhaps the most dramatic example of a team approach to manufacturing established in the United States is at the Romeo, Michigan, plant of the Ford Motor Company. As part of its extensive restructuring program of the past decade, which included an intensive focus on upgrading product quality, Ford has grappled with the problems associated with adopting modern manufacturing techniques using a traditional work force.

The Romeo plant originally produced tractors and went through a shutdown phase that laid off 600 workers. Several years ago, Ford undertook the task of reopening the facility as an automobile engine plant employing the most sophisticated equipment available and using a new work system—team manufacturing. It did so knowing it would have to utilize as many of the former tractor workers as possible. About 65 percent of these workers completed high school. The average employee had worked at the tractor factory for 15 years and averaged 46 years of age. It is estimated that 10 percent were illiterate.

The additional challenge of the plant was to produce an engine of new design using a work force that had never built engines. Moreover, since Ford auto plants are not required to buy components from other Ford plants, the Romeo facility was in competition with others. Romeo management decided to focus on the engine-production accomplishments of Nissan as a set of goals for the reconfigured plant. Accordingly, it set competitive goals: less than 1.5 percent consumer repairs per engine; and 82 percent machine efficiency in the plant (compared to 65 percent in the Ford chain); and cost no higher than Nissan's. Because purchased parts constitute more than half of the engines' cost, Ford also worked with vendors to achieve quality, cost, and delivery targets.

Manufacturing at the Romeo plant is organized around a team structure—everyone at the facility is on a team. Each team has greater responsibility than simply producing a part, or subassembly. Teams are totally responsible for a specific component, such as the engine head, cam or block, and crank. Since there are no central support personnel, each team is responsible for its output and improvements to its output.

A typical team has a lead engineer, three other engineers, a financial analyst, three coordinators, three skilled trades people, and 15 production workers. Team coordinators train new workers, coordinate issues, communicate with other teams, and work on the line when necessary. Workers in the machining area are expected to learn all the jobs on the production line.

They also perform traditional indirect activity, such as tool changes, quality inspection, and some machine repairs. Statistical Process Control information is maintained, either automatically by the machines or by the operators.

Most of the workforce at Romeo was drawn from former Ford employees who had worked at the tractor plant, but certain positions were filled with new hires. Team coordinators, skilled tradespeople, and others were tested to ensure that they had the technical skills to perform their jobs and also the teamwork and leadership skills to operate in the new environment.

Most importantly, Ford made an unusual commitment to workforce training, at least by traditional U.S. standards. Some of the Romeo workforce trained for two years before the first engine was shipped. Training fell into four categories—technical training, vendor training, business training, and team building.

Each worker receives about 150 hours of nontechnical training in addition to the appropriate technical training for his job. Nontechnical training includes team building, general business principles, quality, and computer familiarity. Everyone is connected by electronic mail and data bases are available for Statistical Process Control and for filing reports.

As part of the team approach to manufacturing at Romeo, employees may purchase team uniforms and most do so. As employees complete various training courses, they are rewarded with small, colorful pins especially designed for each course. The pins are worn proudly on the uniforms in the same manner as soldiers wear their combat ribbons.

In April of 1990, the Romeo plant began production after two years of preparation and a $780 million investment. Ford's plunge into new work organization and high levels of training is paying handsomely.

Ford claims that the plant produces the highest-quality auto engines in the world and is the most productive in the United States at 2.04 engines per worker per day. The Romeo plant finishes 98 percent of its machining and assembly operations correctly the first time, nearly double the average rate of 20 years ago.

The plant has only 85 suppliers, compared with 400 at the average engine plant, and has reduced inventory by 50 percent.

There is no quality inspection for incoming parts. In fact, a plant the size of Romeo would normally have 125 inspectors and repairmen—there are none at Romeo. Interestingly, the 225 computers on the shop floor allow manufacturing workers to see the same quality, production, and financial data as the plant manager—workers are part of the team.

A number of other examples in U.S. industry demonstrate the value of nontraditional approaches to manufacturing. Each example shows that U.S. workers can be trained to handle multiple tasks, decision making, and the other skills required of these modern systems.

Service Industries

Work organization in the service sector cannot be formulized. Fast-food restaurants cannot be organized in the same manner as insurance companies or banks. Regardless of the nature of the work system, however, many of the same principles are at work in successful service companies as in reorganized manufacturing companies. These principles are flexible management, more worker training, greater worker empowerment, better worker-manager communications, less paperwork, and fewer supervisors to collect information.

Roughly speaking, there are two types of service organizations: *system-oriented operations*, which depend on a high degree of automation, whether it be computers or automated equipment; and, *people-oriented*, which depend on the ability of workers to please customers personally. In both of these cases, customer service must be the end goal, and people-oriented systems may be heavily backed by automation; but from a customer viewpoint, the two are different.

Many service companies have little or no face-to-face contact with their customers. You may buy a policy from an independent insurance agent and never once in your life meet someone who works for your insurance company. You may utilize Federal Express or United Parcel Service every day and never meet the people who pick up and deliver your packages. Depending on the nature of your banking needs, you may have a little contact with tellers and others in the bank, but you may also have money deposited automatically and just use automatic teller machines.

Other types of service companies depend almost entirely on the perceived service their employees provide. Department stores, restaurants, dry cleaning establishments, speedy printing operations, and other types of retail operations must provide individual service to their customers. Wholesale distributors selling to other businesses combine price with service to please individual owners, or managers. Although these differences exist, when detailing work flow and the nature of customer interfaces, many of the same elements that apply to manufacturing operations become evident.

Although you may never meet someone from your insurance company, you will hear from the company regularly and perhaps call it from time to time. In this case, cheerful, knowledgeable people backed up by useful computer systems can satisfy your relationship and lead you to renew policies and to buy more. Department store personnel must be backed with sophisticated inventory systems and direct mail programs that ensure that inventories are complete for the announced sales. Fast-food restaurants depend on systemized cooking equipment to balance supply with demand minute-by-minute during the day.

In all these examples, worker training is one of the building blocks in the foundation of a new form of work system. Whether a faceless contact is handling your airplane reservation or your mutual fund order, they must understand their products and help you achieve your purchasing goal. Systems must be established to provide them with the information they need, and they must be trained to manipulate the system in a manner to close the sale.

In the case of department stores and other retail establishments, workers must be trained to deal with customers in a manner that reflects the mission of the business. An optimum balance must be reached between efficiency and the time spent with customers; indifference and lack of product knowledge results in lost sales. In fact, in some retail stores selling electronic equipment such as television sets and VCRs, sales people are authorized to negotiate prices with customers. Although this practice is criticized because sales people take advantage of customers who do not have negotiating skills, it represents the ultimate empowerment of workers who deal directly with customers.

That service-sector companies need to improve productivity is apparent. Over the past decade, the service sector of the U.S. economy has shown a decline in output per person. Although much of the service sector is not in competition with foreign companies, profitability has suffered. Much of the effort to upgrade efficiency has focused on white-collar workers in offices that support frontline workers; but, in some cases, it is difficult to distinguish white collar from blue collar in service companies.

Too many service companies have thinned the ranks of indirect workers in an arbitrary attempt to improve profits. This can be dangerous in a service environment. Airlines that reduce reservations personnel, for example, are simply chasing business away. Each situation must be analyzed carefully to ensure efficient work flows.

Motorola views its white-collar staff operations as service companies within the corporation.[6] It studies the work flow in these departments in the same manner it studies manufacturing operations. That is, each white-collar department has a product, customers, raw materials, and cycle times. An example is Motorola's corporate finance department, which must close the company's books each month. In Motorola's case, each month the company has to record 1.3 million credits and debits that occur in operations around the world.[7] By methodically streamlining the process, the company lowered the number of errors and reduced the time it takes to complete the process from eight days to four days, a savings of $20 million each year in professional auditor expense.[8]

In a report in *Fortune* magazine, United Services Automobile Association (USAA)—an insurance and financial investment firm that serves active and retired military officers—disclosed how it has combined high-volume activity with customized customer service to produce satisfaction in the service sector. Although many experts believe the use of computers has been overtouted as a productivity tool, USAA has integrated them with its service representatives in a seamless manner that not only saves time but increases service.[10]

The problem USAA faced about 10 years ago was a declining rate of employee productivity. At that time, the insurance company measured productivity simply by dividing the number of policies in effect by the number of employees who sold and maintained them. Since this formula did not measure customer service, one simple solution to the productivity problem would have been to reduce the number of employees. On the other hand, adding employees to improve service would aggravate the productivity trends. Neither solution was deemed acceptable, so an entirely new measurement scheme was devised, one that included service as well as output-per-person.[11]

An evaluation system called the Family of Measures (FOM) was devised. Now, every month, all 14,000 USAA employees are scored on their performance in quantity, quality, timeliness, and customer service. Each salesperson is a member of a sales team and each team has a FOM record. There is friendly competition and monthly recognition. More importantly, bonuses and promotions are established using the system.[12]

In addition to providing an unusually pleasant working environment, USAA makes sure it backs up workers with plenty of training and automation. The company spends 2.7 percent of its annual payroll on training. Using the most advanced image-processing system in U.S. business, USAA scans all paperwork into a digitized system that uses optical discs for storage. Just one division, the property and casualty insurance division, destroys 99 percent of all its paperwork after it is processed, saving 39,000 square feet of filing cabinets each year.[13]

This digitized system allows customer representatives on the telephone to scan a customer's entire USAA file—auto, home, marine, and other insurance. Additionally, a similar system helps customer-service personnel provide quick answers and quick decisions for investment customers in USAA's mutual fund and annuity business. (USAA only sells products from its central office in San Antonio, Texas—it has no field sales staff.)[14]

The results of USAA's overhaul of work have been startling. The company consistently ranks in the top five of insurance companies for customer satisfaction, its rate of insurance renewals is 99 percent, and it has only quintupled the size of its workforce during a period when its assets grew from $200 million to $19 billion.[15]

First National Bank of Chicago also developed a problem several years ago. When customers contacted the department responsible for issuing letters of credit, they were shuffled from one person to another. It took four days to issue the letter, a delay that sometimes interfered with customer business transactions.[16]

A study of the situation determined that the department was operating exactly as an old-fashioned assembly line operated, with different people in the department responsible for several of the dozen steps it takes to issue a letter of credit. A new process was devised that allowed customers to deal with just one person who was empowered to handle the entire transaction. In fact, whenever customers call for a letter of credit, they are always referred to the same bank representative. Department members were trained so that each person understood the entire process.

The result is that the bank now issues letters of credit the same day they are requested. The number of people in the department has been halved and the number of letters issued annually has doubled—mass production with individualized service.[17]

Through similar service-productivity work reorganizations, coupled with more sophisticated computer systems, American Express's Travel Division has more than doubled its revenues-per-employee the past 10 years, while increasing customer service. For instance, Amex has reduced processing time for new-card applicants by 50 percent, to 11 days.[18]

Still another approach to organizing work is to devise systems that deliver service and then train employees to implement the systems. The classic example of this type of service-sector work system is Federal Express, which devised a nationwide pickup, transit, and delivery service that was so inexpensive and so convenient that it changed the way the United States conducted business.[19] In this case, employees were highly trained to execute intricate schedules, ranging from finely timed pickup of packages at selected locations, to transport to several sites, where hundreds of thousands of packages are sorted and redistributed every night throughout the United States.

Again, here we have high-volume activity combined with customized service. The high volume allows reasonable pricing and the service creates product demand. The FedEx system depends on the absolute performance of trucks that can't break down too often, people who have to pick up on a precise schedule, airplanes that work, a mammoth sorting system, and then a mirror-image delivery cycle beginning early in the morning every day. Additionally, every package is tracked by a computer system so that customers can check on its progress.[20]

To make this system work, Federal Express and other companies in the same business have provided an unusual amount of incentive and training. In this case, employee interface with customers is less important than execution of the system, but training is no less important.

Finally, one must consider the success of the Nordstrom department store chain. Although Nordstrom is automated as much as any large-volume business must be, customer interface makes it the most successful chain in the industry. Although it has 64 stores coast-to-coast and over $2.5 billion in annual sales, Nordstrom has established a high degree of customized service as its comparative advantage.[21] In effect, Nordstrom's management determined that there is a market segment that will pay top dollar for products sold with a high degree of customer assistance.

Accordingly, customer representatives in the Seattle-based company receive comprehensive training before they are exposed to customers, and they must demonstrate expertise in the particular section of the store in which they work.

The store is legendary for the extraordinary steps its salespeople take to satisfy a customer. Salespeople are authorized to stay with a customer as he or she goes from department to department to assemble an ensemble. Shoes are dyed and decorated to match a dress.

In this example, employee training and empowerment come first because Nordstrom's management recognized that its product is, in fact, service, not clothing. Anyone can build a department store and buy merchandise to fill it, but there must be a match between target prospects, price, and service that makes strategic sense. Many department-store chains are struggling with high levels of debt incurred through leveraged buyouts in the 1980s; others are struggling with the spread of low-price competitors. Stores that pretend to be traditional full-service establishments but don't provide a matching measure of service are doomed to failure.

An additional point: Nordstrom employees are not competing for their jobs with foreign work forces, but management deliberately selected a strategy of raising profits by increasing the value-added component of their employees.

The key to establishing an efficient work system—in manufacturing or service businesses—begins with a sensible business strategy that then combines the right mixture of training, automation, and employee selection. Those businesses that can benefit from employee empowerment—whether for the purpose of providing customer service or for the purpose of building products efficiently—must concoct this blend in a customized manner.

In creating this formula, however, certain generic considerations must be overlaid on the organization to ensure the success of these new approaches.

A concept of total quality must be instilled in the workforce, both in the service sector and in manufacturing. At times, to separate quality from work organization is difficult, but it must be approached separately if high levels of quality are to be expected. Employees must understand the effects of low-quality output on their performance and on the business success of the enterprise. They must comprehend the linkages between their output and their fellow workers' output. They must learn that there are no efficiency, no margins, no profits, and no pay without quality.

By the same token, vendors must adopt the same attitudes if they are to become suppliers that don't interfere with a company's quality goals. This may mean backward integration of training, exchanges of employees, and other techniques that produce results. Many large companies now require their vendors to apply for the Malcolm Baldrige National Quality Award each year because the application process itself provides management with good insight into company strengths and weaknesses.

Just-in-time delivery systems not only reduce inventory costs, but they instill discipline in the work process and cause vendors to reorganize their work systems. JIT applies to service as well as to manufacturing operations—whether timely delivery of groceries for a restaurant, which eliminates the cost of a second refrigerator, or timely delivery of other merchandise, which reduces working-capital needs.

One of the fallouts of new work systems is a blurring of wage and salary work. Blurring can be a problem with organizations whose cultures have labored for decades to ensure there is a distinction. The differences range from pay scales, to perquisites, to what people wear to work. In systems where all types of workers tend to work more closely, and where a goal is to establish teamwork, these traditional barriers can be troublesome. Depending on the circumstances, management must devise techniques to break down barriers but maintain appropriate compensation differentials.

Some companies have used sports analogies to rationalize these differences. Most workers understand the difference between the quarterback and an interior lineman. Both are critical for success, but normally the quarterback is paid more and recognized as the team leader on the field. In the end, however, higher-paid, exempt workers—like quarterbacks—must demonstrate their worth to the team, or resentment will fester.

The entire subject of compensation takes a turn when new work systems are installed. To the extent that workers are asked to undertake additional responsibilities, inevitably, they will expect higher pay; to the extent that a new work system produces higher profits, workers should share them. The problem to avoid in this situation is establishing unrealistic expectations. To that end, many companies have discovered that the more employees understand the business they are in, the better insight they have into the possibilities. This might include an insight into their markets and the activities of competitors.

In recognition of their ability to affect profits directly, a number of companies have begun to provide frontline workers with compensation systems traditionally reserved for executives. Nucor Company, a manufacturer of specialty steel products, ties every employee's salary to productivity and job performance. Their base salaries are below the industry average but workers can earn 50 or 60 percent more if their work team performs well. Earnings are calculated and paid weekly, according to business results.

DuPont pays the 20,000 employees in its fibers business 6 percent less than its workers in other units. If the unit meets its profit targets, the employees are paid an additional 6 percent. If profits reach up to 150 percent of target, employees receive up to an additional 12 percent.[22]

In some cases, skills upgrading might be rewarded with higher pay. When General Motors reorganized its Cadillac Division engine plant into a team manufacturing system, the company installed a compensation system that rewards workers for becoming qualified to perform a wider range of activities.[23] The incentive system accelerated learning and the ability of the workers to perform in the new environment. The plant reached the breakeven point a year ahead of plan, and its performance helped Cadillac win one of the 1990 Malcolm Baldrige National Quality Awards.[24] In any case, compensation merits a great deal of advance thought and, perhaps, consultation with a specialist.

Finally, new ways of organizing work need new ways of determining what is going on in the workplace and new forms of control. Management should ensure that empowered frontline workers have current and insightful feedback regarding their activity. Thus, in a manufacturing operation where teams are handling multiprocess activities, members of the team should have a feedback system to let engineers and others know about necessary design changes and other activities that are impinging on their success. In a retail operation, customer reactions are important.

This feedback mechanism can be computer based or simply take the form of frequent meetings. Not only will management receive firsthand information from these reporting systems, the systems will fulfill a need empowered employees have for carrying out their new responsibilities to the organization.

In the area of control, management must establish information systems of some sort to replace the layers of supervisors that new work systems eliminate. In the Taylor model, each layer of supervisors has a layer of personal responsibility that he can implement regarding problems and decisions, with information moving up the strata according to the seriousness of the problem or question. When these layers are removed and employees are empowered, an information and control vacuum is created.

Since management cannot abandon its responsibility for overall control, a system must be installed to provide information even as employees are told they have control of the work process. Usually, the employee-feedback mechanism is also the control system. In a perfect world, each step of a manufacturing process would be captured by computers and integrated instantly throughout the plant, thus providing management with total control at all times. That is, information about work-in-process, inventory, quality, and scheduling all would flow to management under the guise of employee reporting.

However these systems are established, new work organization cannot be achieved without thoughtful, strategic planning. Underpinning all efforts to achieve these productivity breakthroughs is faith in the U.S. worker—faith that he and she can be trained to achieve complex tasks; faith that U.S. business cannot be successful unless it undertakes a high-skill, high-wage strategy; faith that the U.S. economy depends on the wealth of the U.S. worker.

In developing strategies for closing the work-organization gap, business should also look to the government for policy changes that will facilitate change. Government assistance ranges from leadership and motivation to direct help in the form of technical training and tax relief.

The final chapter of this book outlines the role business must play in developing these public-policy programs.

VALUE-ADDED WORK ORGANIZATIONS CHECKLIST

1. Product definition—Despite what may seem to be obvious, determine what you are really selling. Are you selling a unique product or service that can be priced high because you are the only producer? Are you selling a commodity product that competes for the most part on the basis of price? Are you selling widgets or selling the delivery of widgets? Do you depend on a well-implemented product-delivery system to achieve success, or does success depend more on the interface between your employees and your customers? If both, assign percentages.

2. Workforce analysis—How could your workforce add more value to your product to give you a marketing edge? Could it reduce costs, increase quality, increase speed of delivery, improve product design? Don't limit your thinking because of your opinions of your workers. Presume you have an ideal workforce.

3. Work-organization analysis—Design a new work organization that would allow workers to add additional value to the product. Involve as many workers in this process as possible. They know where the production problems reside. Do not conduct this analysis with preconceived ideas of the workforce's capabilities. Design an ideal work environment that will produce the results you desire, including as much decentralization of decision making to frontline workers as necessary.

4. Workforce evaluation—What does your employee profile look like? How much education and training do they have? What sort of personal problems are impinging on their effectiveness (single parents with children have constraints, for example)?

5. Employee training analysis—Combine the assumptions of your new workplace environment with your employee profile, and determine in detail the type and amount of training the workforce will need to implement the new work organization. Ask your workers to evaluate the training curriculum and make suggestions. Produce detailed schedules of the type of training in the appropriate sequence for each type of job. Include remedial reading, writing, and math training for those that need it.

Provide leadership training for those who need it. Detail the introduction of the new system.

6. Ancillary workforce systems—Determine how compensation must change to motivate employees and to reward them for undertaking additional responsibilities. If necessary, explain the new differences between white-collar and blue-collar workers.

7. Ancillary workplace systems—Determine schedules for phasing in just-in-time delivery systems with vendors and within the work organization; schedule quality improvement targets and work with vendors to meet them; establish continuous improvement systems. Involve the workforce in this activity, including contact with vendor workers.

8. Communications—Work out a detailed communications program to introduce the changes to the workforce. Explain what's in it for the workforce. Establish a business feedback system so that everyone knows how the changes are progressing against plan and how successful the changes are. Make sure that expectations are realistic.

9. Implement.

CHAPTER 7

CLOSING THE
TRAINING GAP

During the early months of 1990, the value and potential of America's youths were demonstrated night after night on television screens throughout the world. Nineteen and 20-year-old men and women shot down scud missiles with sophisticated Patriot missile batteries, maintained ultra high-tech aircraft, cleared mine fields, and engaged in tank combat without direction.

One of the great demonstrations of the Gulf War was that young Americans from all backgrounds can quickly make the transition from the youthful indulgences of high school to responsible adulthood, given the proper motivation, training, and adult example. It is a lesson mainstream adults—teachers, employers, parents, union leaders—have yet to absorb.

The demand for skilled workers in the U.S. civilian workforce is qualitatively different from previous skills shortages. Rapid changes in technology mandate continuous systematic lifelong learning, rather than the more traditional single period of occupational preparation. And the education and training of new workers is not keeping up with changing demand. Knowledge and skills requirements call for more than high school education alone. Formal learning will have to be supplemented by continuous learning throughout working life as technology, consumer preferences, and trade patterns continue to shift.

Labor-force participation in the United States has reached a new high of 67 percent.[1] Combined with the effect of demographic trends, this means employers will find it increasingly difficult to find workers during the decade ahead. This all adds up to a heightened need to train current U.S. workers so that they become more productive. Training will also continue to be important due to the mobility of the nation's workforce. At least 15 percent of the workforce needs to be retrained each year just due to turnover.

There are three components in the continuum of life-long readiness for work: (1) basic education, including practical work experience during the final few years of academic preparation; (2) career-long on-the-job training, including training in the workplace and at community facilities; and (3) periodic retraining for those whose skills become obsolete, who lose their jobs or need special training because they are disadvantaged.

These three components are heavily dependent on establishment of a public/private partnership that operates on a national scale. The nation's education system must include work orientation in its current restructuring activity. Existing governmental programs must be coordinated, focused, and include a business component. Public-sector institutions, such as community colleges, must become even more involved with post-employment training.

The essence of this change in the United States is reorientation of existing programs and institutions to recognize the importance of workforce training. Business must become the leading advocate for this change and then must follow through with practical programs to demonstrate the benefits. America's youth must not be forced to drift, and U.S. workers must be trained to reach their potential.

There are several essential components of a New American Training System:

1. A high school/business relationship that starts the majority of our youth down a skills-training road, resulting in high-paying jobs.

2. A community college/technical college business relationship that continues to train high school graduates for high-paying jobs.

3. On-the-job, life-long training that may utilize public training institutions and private proprietary institutions as resources.

4. A business/public partnership organization that coordinates all training in a community to meet business and worker needs.

These components of a new U.S. worker-preparation system will take years to establish on a nationwide basis, but business must begin advocating now for the changes that will make it possible. Fortunately, pieces of the system are already in place or are being experimented with, and there are a great many advocates for organizing the effort. Those elements already existing, such as the community college system, are ready to help employers upgrade the skills of their workers now.

The United States has what can best be described as a do-it-yourself school-to-work transition system. For the approximately 20 million 16-to-24-year-olds who are unlikely to enter college, life is too often a matter of bouncing from one part-time or temporary job to another until, in their mid-20s, an employer decides they are seasoned enough to be treated seriously.[2]

Until recently, the nation's schools have accepted little responsibility for the fate of noncollege-bound students after they left the classroom. Employers blame the schools for poor academic preparation and lax work habits, but have little contact with the schools themselves and provide little in the way of structured training for either the students or recent graduates they hire. Many employers simply avoid hiring young people entirely.

The dilemma these young people face is more than a social problem; it is a basic business problem. The 1980s saw an historic increase in the workplace.[3] Until the mid-1970s, about 60 percent of the population participated in the workforce. Now, two thirds are working. But the supply of skilled new workers is not keeping up with the potential demand.

In aggregate terms, the number of young people available to enter the labor force each year has declined by three million in the last five years and will remain well below recent levels through the year 2000.[4] Between 1980 and 1996, the youth population—age 15 to 24—is expected to fall 21 percent, from about 43 to 34 million.[5]

In addition to lower numbers of new entrants, the labor force will have quite a different composition over the next decade. For instance, the majority of new workers will be women, minorities, and immigrants—groups that have traditionally had lower educational attainment or more-limited occupational preparation than have native white males.[6] It is also expected that many of the new entrants will opt for temporary, part-time, homebound, or shared employment.[7] This changing nature of the supply will present unprecedented challenges to meet the demand for skilled workers.

These skill shortages will not occur in low-paying jobs or professional ends of the spectrum. They will be in the middle ground where formal education and work-based training beyond high school are required. In transportation, banking, health services, computer services, and most of the other rapidly growing service industries, labor shortages are already occurring in those jobs requiring solid academic skills combined with job-specific training.

There are no reliable statistics regarding the amount of training the U.S. workforce receives, neither on the job nor during the preemployment phase of life. Few records are kept by businesses and those that do so follow no uniform system. Public-sector institutions keep records but they have no way of knowing how their training is used. This lack of information reflects society's attitude toward the subject—that training is a private matter between employers and their employees.

Available data imply that business spends between $30 billion and $44 billion annually on training of all types for all levels of employees.[8] Annually, this would be a range of 1.2 percent and 1.8 percent of the total U.S. payroll of $2.4 trillion.[9] If accurate, this percentage would rank U.S. workers among poorest trained among industrialized nations, at least as expressed in percentage of payroll spent.

In any case, averages don't tell the story—training is uneven, and, depending on the size of the company you work for and your particular job, you may receive quite a bit of training or none at all. Surveys do demonstrate that certain categories of jobs receive more training than others and that larger companies provide more training and smaller companies.[10]

The value of worker training has been demonstrated over and over. According to *Training* magazine, a publication of the American Society of Training and Development (ASTD), employee training accounted for more than half of the nation's productivity gains during the past several decades.[11] McKinsey & Co., a consulting company, recently studied 39 companies in England that manufacture machine tools to determine the distinctions between successful and less successful operations. Among other findings, the study discovered that the best-performing firms had fewer managers, a higher proportion of skilled workers, and that they spent six times more per employee on education and training. The best companies were more productive.[12]

The principal difficulty in describing the status of worker training in the United States, however, is the lack of an education-and-training continuum. That is, high school students disappear from the statistical radar screen at about age 16 and then reappear at various points during the following 10 years, at which time they can be counted as a permanent member of the workforce. Lacking a cohesive attitude towards work, education, and training, the United States has difficulty describing its problem and, therefore, finding a solution.

As a result, the saga of an average American worker during the past two decades appears to have followed this sequence:

1. Bored with high school and noting that graduates aren't paid more than dropouts, our American Worker leaves school at age 17 and gets a full-time job in the fast-food restaurant in which he has worked part-time for the previous two years (minimum wage plus 50 cents per hour and no health benefits).

2. During the following eight years, American Worker drifts from job to job seeking higher wages. Employers offer these jobs based on the growing maturity and stability of the worker, not on acquired skills. (At age 25, American Worker earns $6.25 per hour and has some benefits, such as vacations and contributory medical insurance. Companies are motivated to hire younger workers to minimize health insurance costs.)

3. At age 26, American Worker marries and realizes that he must learn a skill that qualifies him for a higher-paying job and benefits needed by a family. American Worker enrolls for classes at a community college or a professional technical school.

4. At age 28, our worker finds semiskilled employment with a large company. (Pay is $8.75 per hour and a full range of benefits that adds $2.50 cents per hour to the employer's direct-wage costs.)

5. At age 38, American Worker has survived a company downsizing because of good work habits, dependability, and average skill competency. Through on-the-job training, American Worker has learned to operate a particular numerically controlled (NC) machine and is now paid $13 per hour. With two children at home and a wife with a part-time job, conditions are pretty good. (Even with the addition of a part-time wage earner, however, there are no savings for the children's college or an emergency reserve. Retirement and medical benefits are based entirely on the primary wage earner's company programs.)

6. At age 48, American Worker is laid off as part of a comprehensive retrenchment at his company, which has steadily lost market share to Japanese companies for the past 10 years. (Our worker has 20 years service and will be eligible for a pension in another 15 years.)

7. Although Worker is quite skilled at operating one or two numerically controlled machines, he cannot qualify for any other job that pay $13 per hour, and there are no open positions requiring this particular skill. After exhausting unemployment benefits, Worker accepts a job as a security guard at $8 per hour because it also offers medical benefits. American Worker's spouse takes a full-time job at $6 per hour in a department store. Both are unqualified for all skilled jobs that appear in their locale.

The key missing ingredient to this tragic scenario is a lack of continuous education and training—American Worker's company failed to upgrade his skills so that it could compete with more-efficient Japanese producers, and he was set adrift at what should have been the most productive period of his life.

One way to think about closing this gap is to view an idealized work path for our hypothetical American Worker:

1. At age 16, American Worker and his parents have an extensive interview with a trained counselor form the U.S. Employment Service. They determine that our worker does not wish to attend college, but is motivated to learn a skill and undertake a career in manufacturing.

2. American Worker is interviewed by several local manufacturers and one of them offers him a part-time job working on the factory floor. The manufacturing company tells American Worker that a full-time job awaits but that he must obtain a high school diploma. The part-time job includes routine duties that familiarize the worker with the manufacturing environment, which he learns from experienced workers throughout the factory. He receives course credits and grades from his high school for this work experience. (The part-time job pays minimum wage.)

3. At age 18, Worker receives a high school diploma and works at the manufacturing company 20 hours per week as a second-step apprentice. A condition of continuing employment is enrollment at a technical community college for two years, which leads to an Associate Degree in Manufacturing Technology. At work, the worker is assigned to learn how to operate a specific numerically controlled (NC) machine through direct on-the-job training. At the community college, he is taught theory—such as statistical process control, total quality management, and business finance—plus practical manufacturing knowledge, such as NC tool maintenance and operation. (Starting wage for a second-step apprentice is twice minimum wage, and there is a contributory medical program. The employer is motivated to retain older workers and to minimize employee turnover because the operation is based on a high degree of employee involvement in operations, which places a premium on experience and skill.)

4. At age 20, American Worker receives an associate degree and completes the apprentice phase. American Worker becomes the junior member of a work team assigned to produce a complex component used in an automobile assembly. The team is responsible for design, production, and quality of the assembly. It has its own tools and is responsible for unit costs; it works with three vendors who deliver parts to the factory based on schedules established by the team. During the next five years, American Worker learns how to operate all seven of the machines used to produce the component and also learns inventory and work-in-process control techniques, communications skills needed to operate within the team and with vendors, and how to compute costs for a bill of materials. For four hours each month, after work, he attends classes in the factory. Sometimes, vendors appear at these sessions to update workers on new technologies, and, at other times, management updates workers on the business. (American Worker now earns 250 percent of the minimum wage and is eligible for bonuses based on the performance of the factory and on the performance of his work team.)

5. Over the following 20 years, American Worker learns all the skills on the factory floor. He is offered one of the few exempt supervisory positions in the factory several times but declines because of the demands on the time of these personnel. Periodically, American Worker experiences intense periods of training as technology changes cause new machines to replace old machines and as customer products undergo change. He becomes an expert at training vendors to meet factory demands. At one point, he returns to the technical community college as a full-time student for three months at the expense of the employer to study the operations of computers. (By age 48, American Worker is earning $55,000 annually, including bonuses and wages.)

This version of the American Worker saga could unfold in several directions, but chances are that this particular company will be successful and our worker will have a life-long job in concert with his or her life-long learning experience. If for some reason this particular American Worker is laid off, he or she should have little trouble finding employment.

In this idealized situation, there are a number of alterations to life as experienced by most current U.S. workers.

- High school students are helped to identify their career aspirations and then fitted into a system that helps them to achieve appropriate career training.
- There is a tangible association between a local high school, a community college, and local employers.

- A visible sequence of progress occurs between public education, post-secondary education, and work, with milestones and rewards—all of which are important to young people who need help and feedback during this critical period of their lives.
- Employees have a commitment to life-long learning and training that benefit workers as well as businesses.
- There is a work system that can exploit the abilities of well-trained workers.

Business people have multiple roles in helping to create this environment for workers. In addition to helping the education system improve academic performance, business people must establish the linkages to high schools that help young people comprehend the association of education and work. Public policies must be reshaped at the federal, state, and local levels to include available government resources in the equation, including community colleges, the U.S. Employment Service, and agencies devoted to helping disadvantaged and displaced workers. Finally, business must devote additional resources to worker training and adopt work systems that take advantage of capable employees.

These changes require a new cultural attitude in the United States regarding work. In other nations, training and business-public partnerships are the product of national consensus, and it is unlikely that business can achieve the requisite transformation in the United States without similar consensus. The U.S. education system is undergoing change, but the process could be accelerated if the public understood the linkages between a well-educated workforce and the nation's standard of living. Business can upgrade internal training and effect organizational change without public permission, but help from the public sector would speed this transition, particularly for smaller businesses. The major initiative not yet launched is the school-to-work system.

Roughly speaking, over the next decade the United States will need 25 percent of its workers to have four-year college degrees or higher; another 50 percent should have more than a high school degree but less than a bachelor's degree; the remainder will work in jobs that don't require much skill.[13]

U.S. business is suffering because the middle 50 percent of its workers are not skilled enough to handle new work organizations and new technologies. For this group we must erect a new mechanism for work preparation. In the meantime, business must upgrade the current workforce. Fortunately, there are overlaps between the system of the future and the system of the present and, therefore, promise that the nation can achieve short-range as well as long-range worker-preparation goals.

The United States needs a home-built apprentice system aimed at students who don't attend college. At the moment, 56 percent of high school graduates are enrolled in two-year or four-year colleges the same year they graduate, but only half of those will eventually earn their degrees.[14] It's likely that if students were given clear-cut alternatives to college—alternatives that promised high-paying careers, fewer would pursue so-called academic tracks in high school. As things now stand, jobs requiring college degrees are so much better compensated than jobs requiring only high school diplomas that students are encouraged to continue their education. The United States must establish worthwhile alternatives.

As part of the widespread activity underway in the United States to upgrade the education system, there is discussion regarding a firmer link between high school curricula and the needs business have for productive workers. There has been a vocational education system in U.S. public schools since 1917.[15] In fact, the system was started by the U.S. Chamber of Commerce during an earlier period of skilled-worker shortage. This traditional system, however, is no longer a satisfactory supplier of skilled workers. Most vocational education students don't pursue careers in the fields they study, and there is little coordination between the needs of local employers and the schools.[16]

Although the United States should not attempt to implement the rigid systems utilized in other countries to prepare their youth for work—as outlined in Chapter 3—the nation must embrace the notion that business and education should collaborate to help students become trained for good jobs.

There are a number of programs and experiments to achieve this linkage. Although most of them were started to serve at-risk youth who are probable dropouts, they do demonstrate that work-related courses and activities can be integrated into high schools.

The National Alliance of Business, with a grant from the Department of Labor, is managing a program in conjunction with the Bank of America and Sears, Roebuck Company to integrate high school and work. Called the Quality Connection, the program is preparing students in San Francisco for bank jobs, and students in Illinois for positions as appliance-repair personnel.[17] High schools in these locations have agreed to alter their curricula to include courses that are useful to the students' part-time jobs. The purpose of the Quality Connection project is to determine how business and education can work together to smooth the transition from school to work.

The Jobs for America's Graduates (JAGS) program is serving 12,000 students each year in over 275 high schools in 13 states.[18] Aimed at high school seniors, this program, during the past five years, has placed 85 percent of them in jobs or in additional training and schooling. The national board of JAGS is composed of elected officials, educators, business people, and labor leaders. The program is financed by funds from the Job Training Partnership Act.

The Croom Vocational High School in New Carrolton, Maryland, represents a dedicated vocational school. To enter the school, a student must be certified to be "at-risk" of dropping out. Nearly all students in the school have poor grades and many have dropped out at least once.

Croom students spend half of each day in vocational programs, and they maintain all the facilities at the school. They prepare cafeteria meals, operate day-care centers for small children and the elderly, and they operate an auto repair shop, which is open to the public. The other half of the day is spent in class on academic subjects. Because of the focus at Croom, and the dedication of the staff, the school has an unusually successful record of helping at-risk youth.

But the United States needs a mechanism for preparing all noncollege-bound youth for work, not just the disadvantaged.

The nation needs an integrated career-preparation system that seamlessly connects high school, advanced-skills training, and work. Two traditional systems—vocational schools and apprenticeships—have not met their potential.

The Carl D. Perkins Vocational Educational Act was first passed in 1984 and reauthorized in 1990. The law currently provides nearly $1.0 billion annually, with about 80 percent going directly to the states for training. The states use about 40 percent of their funds for adult training at post-secondary educational institutions.[19]

The Perkins Act also provides funds to the states for a number of programs aimed at demonstrating the effectiveness of school-to-work transition activity. Included in these programs is tech-prep, which integrates the last two years of high school with an additional two years of vocational training and other cooperative efforts between business, labor, and education.

Additionally, the new law supports development of national standards for various competencies in various industries and trades. Grants are available to trade associations and to labor organizations for organizing business-labor-education committees that would determine standards.

Another traditional system—apprenticeships—plays a minor role in the nation's random scheme for career preparation. About 300,000 people are enrolled in apprenticeship programs, which is about .16 percent of the U.S. workforce.[20] In Germany, 6 percent of the workforce is enrolled in these programs.[21] Moreover, during the past 20 years, the percentage of apprentices in the U.S. workforce has declined substantially.[22]

More than half of U.S. apprentices work in unionized construction and manufacturing operations, so the decline in enrollment has paralleled the decline in union membership.[23] Although nonunion apprenticeship programs may be formed, the costs of attending classes, on-the-job training, and testing are fairly significant. Accordingly, many unions negotiate for apprentice programs as part of their bargaining. By the same token, when an industry or company enters a difficult economic period, unions have allowed them to reduce or eliminate such programs.

In any case, with the median age of apprentices at 25, the system has never been a true school-to-work pathway.[24]

These two traditional systems—vocational education and apprenticeships—are weak vehicles for preparing students for the workplace. Although the apprenticeship programs supplying skilled craftsmen to the building trades remains effective, it is not feasible to strengthen and expand this concept so that it becomes the main provider of skilled workers. Similarly, the nation's vocational education system is limited in the number and quality of skills training it can deliver. Accordingly, these two approaches should be abandoned except where they are useful for particular careers. They must be augmented with a new approach.

One of the strengths of career systems utilized in Western Europe is widespread recognition of certified career training. In Germany, for example, there are over 400 different job-certification careers that youths can learn through the nation's apprenticeship programs.[25] In these systems, employees receive certificates attesting to the fact that they have taken certain academic and skill training and have demonstrated capabilities at a particular standard. In the United States, a number of professional occupations are certified, such as doctors, lawyers, and accountants; and some skilled jobs are certified, such as electricians, plumbers, and carpenters.

Certification has the advantage of ensuring that a body of knowledge and skill has been acquired. Additionally, certification allows portability, an important asset for workers and employers alike in a nation with as mobile a workforce as the United States.

The United States needs a national certification program for a broad range of frontline worker skills. Business needs assurance that new workers have been trained to world-class standards. There are a number of ways to implement a national certification program, some of which are already in use. Trade associations could design curricula and practical work-experience programs that lead to certification. Consortia of businesses could be formed to design certification criteria for specific entry-level jobs. Colleges and universities could design such programs under contract to associations and other industry groups. Employers and their unions could join forces to design certification programs. The federal government could play a leading role in determining basic certification criteria. As the business community leads the way in developing definitions for needed skills, it can also take advantage of the activity already underway in this area.

The Vocational Technical Education Consortium of States has developed descriptions of the tasks involved for over 250 different occupations.[26] The National Occupational Competencies Testing Institute has established assessment standards for 69 occupations.[27] Other organizations are studying this topic, including the Educational Testing Service, American Institutes for Research, the Center for Occupational Research and Development, the National Assessment Institute, and the Mid-America Vocational Curriculum Consortia.[28]

The federal government has also demonstrated interest in occupational definitions. The Carl D. Perkins Vocational and Applied Technology Education Act Amendments require every state to develop standards for vocational education by 1992. The U.S. Department of Labor maintains a Dictionary of Occupational Titles and is currently revising it.

In 1990, the U.S. Secretary of Labor established a new commission—the Secretary's Commission on Achieving Necessary Skills (SCANS)—which was charged with recommending a set of worker competencies that business needs other than the traditional academic skills of reading, writing, and arithmetic. In June 1991, the Commission issued an interim report that identified five basic competencies:

1. The ability to allocate resources, such as time, money, and materials.
2. Good interpersonal skills that allow workers to work on teams, to teach others, to serve customers.
3. The ability to acquire and evaluate information and data, including the ability to use computers.
4. The ability to monitor and to evaluate systems and performance so that they can be improved.
5. The ability to utilize technology and tools.

Complementing these competencies are three other characteristics that the Commission believes are needed for workplace achievement: (1) basic skills, such as reading, writing, arithmetic, speaking, and listening; (2) thinking skills, such as creativity, decision making, problem solving; and (3) personal qualities, such as individual responsibility, self-esteem, and integrity.

The SCANS Commission is seeking the endorsement of the business community for these characteristics and competencies and the agreement of the education community that they will be taught and inculcated in the school system. The Commission believes that schools should issue a certificate of mastery to students so they can prove to prospective employers that they have achieved these traits. This would be a basic level of certification for workers.

In the private sector, it's estimated that about 200 trade and professional associations have established programs to assess and certify the skills of individuals in specific occupations. The American Institute of Banking, a subsidiary of the American Banking Association, trains about 300,000 workers each year and offers three levels of accreditation in banking skills.[29] The National Tooling and Machining Association has trained workers since 1943, when it was formed to replace machinists drafted into the war effort.[30] A number of employer-union programs also produce certified craftsmen.

Despite the long history of certification in the United States, the number of frontline workers who actually hold occupational certificates is small. Because of the mobility of the workforce and the minimum amount of training frontline workers receive in the United States, employers confront an unusual amount of turnover without standard gauges for hiring; it is difficult to measure a worker's skills based on prior employment. This situation contributes to the slowness U.S. business has demonstrated in adopting new work organizations.

Accordingly, business must become an advocate for national certification of skills. Because the very nature of modern work organizations agitates against narrowly defined skills, however, it would be a mistake to approach standard setting entirely on the basis of occupations. Modern factories and stores need workers who can handle multiple assignments.

The Commission on the Skills of the American Workforce has recommended that the Secretary of Labor establish a National Board for Professional and Technical Standards. The board would be composed of representatives from employers, labor, and education for the purpose of developing a national system of industry-based standards that would lead to certification.[31] The U.S. Office of Technology Assessment has recommended that federal funds be used as seed money for establishing an Employer Institute for Work-Based Learning, which could address standards as well as industry training practices.[32]

Because training is delivered at the local level, with a particularly important role by community and technical colleges, the states must also have a role in certification. As mentioned earlier, the Perkins Act Amendments of 1990 specify that some of these funds should be used by the states for integration of academic and vocational curricula and for support of so-called tech-prep partnerships.

Many people believe the tech-prep, or "two plus two" approach to skills training is the ideal American version of the European school-to-work model for workers who do not pursue a four-year college degree. The system calls for a true collaboration between a number of sectors in an average community.

Essentially, the tech-prep system is a four-year regimen for skills training, which includes the final two years of high school and an additional two years of training in a local community or technical college. Some versions have students working during some or all of this period with specified employers in a quasi-apprenticeship system; the specifics of a classroom-workplace mix would probably depend on a particular occupational career and the nature of the local collaborative that establishes the program.

The strength of this system is that it is managed by a community collaborative with focus on the needs of local employers. Students do not undertake training in a vacuum in hope that an employer has need for their skills—they are offered training for jobs that exist. Students with a particular affinity for careers that are not available in their hometowns would have the opportunity to study in other communities where the community college offers their preference.

There are over 1,200 community and technical colleges in the United States, most of which already have experience working with business.[33] A business-high school-college relationship is a short step to take in establishing a meaningful school-to-work transition system in the United States.

This collaborative must agree to offer noncollege-bound students better education alternatives. The business community must identify the advantages of the alternatives by demonstrating specific needs for trained people. Boundaries must be established between high school and community colleges, between school and part-time work, and between school and parents.

Eventually, curricula must be established for the clusters of skills that have been identified to be in short supply. This must include a blend of academic and practical courses that meet the needs of a well-rounded student—there must not be too much emphasis on career training. American students and parents will insist on the right of students to change their minds and to continue an academic career, so this alternative cannot be obviated by a lack of courses in basic academic matters.

A heavy degree of student counseling must accompany this sort of program. Counselors must help students and parents determine career choices and then follow students carefully to ensure that they are meeting their goals.

Finally, a marketing program must be implemented to sell the community on the concept. The tech-prep concept is new enough in this country that objections and fears may be raised, so it is important to anticipate controversy.

Business has an important role in establishing this system. It must agitate for cooperation between the public school system and community colleges; it must establish the need for better-prepared students, including the rewards that will accrue to those who are trained; it must help organize and oversee a community collaborative; it must work with students during the period they are undergoing preparation for work, including hiring them in part-time jobs.

Community colleges are ready to participate in this new partnership and to a large extent are already an important facet of the nation's training system. Since 1970, enrollment in community colleges and technical schools has grown by 350 percent and nearly 700 new institutions have been established.[34] In 1988, there were 4.6 million students enrolled in publicly supported two-year colleges and approximately 260,000 additional people enrolled in private, proprietary technical schools.[35]

Surveys indicate that only one third of the students in publicly supported two-year colleges plan to transfer to four-year colleges and receive a baccalaureate degree, and only half of them then do so.[36] More than half of these students in two-year institutions are over the age of 25, and more than a third are over age 30; the average is 29.[37] These statistics suggest that two-year community colleges are principally serving people who have decided to advance their career possibilities by voluntarily returning to school and that there is not an organized system for utilizing these institutions for the nation's youth.

Employers have also discovered the potential of two-year community colleges and have turned to them more and more as a source of advanced training for their employees. Nearly 75 percent of the nation's 1,200 community colleges and technical schools provide customized training to local businesses.[38] Thus, as business tries to build a coordinated national system of skills certification and school-to-work activity, it also has at hand a potentially powerful resource for upgrading the quality of the current workforce.

Community and technical colleges are operated by the states and represent just one example of a growing state involvement with worker training. States have become more involved with training for employees, in some cases using community and technical colleges. In 1989, 44 states operated one or more customized training programs for businesses, costing an aggregate of $375 million.[39] Of the 51 projects identified in these state projects, 19 were conducted in local two-year colleges.[40]

For example, in 1986, International Business Machines (IBM) decided to shift the mission of its Boulder, Colorado, facility from manufacturing to development of computer software.[41]

The company enlisted the help of Front Range Community College to retrain 1,200 of the 2,000 employees at the facility and continues to use the college for ongoing employee training.[42]

Clearly, community colleges could be a valuable resource for businesses throughout the nation. The institutions are located in over 1,200 communities, with close association to local labor markets. However, there is a serious obstacle to overcome before business can exploit this resource for preparation of high school youth and for continuing training of current employees. Community colleges must be recognized by their states and by accrediting organizations for the occupational training they provide for business as well as for individuals.

Most community colleges have evolved over the years to serve their communities in a variety of ways, including some occupational training for individuals and for businesses. Most states fund these institutions, however, based on full-time equivalent (FTE) enrollments, which is the same formula used for four-year colleges and universities. Accordingly, the two-year schools do not receive funds from most states for the short courses that many employers need; nor are these courses recognized by accrediting bodies when they consider a college's status. Colorado community colleges, for example, must provide courses that last at least 15 hours and use a standard curriculum in order to be reimbursed for a student.[43]

For these reasons, when helping business with its training problems, community colleges typically seek self-funded, large classes through contracts, which inevitably means that only larger employers can afford to use them.

There are several examples of how these institutions can be effective when states and the federal government recognize their potential. The Southern Technology Council, composed of representatives from southern state governments and businesses, established the Consortium for Manufacturing Competitiveness (CMC) in 1988.[44] Using 14 educational institutions throughout the area, the CMC is demonstrating that community colleges can help manufacturers with new technology and produce graduates who are technologically prepared.[45] Business not only advises the consortium, but provides funds for specialized equipment.[46]

This project will enhance the manufacturing capability of the southern region and will also establish community colleges in the area as good sources of manufacturing employees, but it falls short of institutionalizing two-year colleges as a standard source of training for individuals and for local businesses.

In South Carolina, each of the state's 16 technical colleges has a full-time workplace specialist who works as a consultant to local businesses.[47] Since 1988, this program has identified over 30,000 workers who need basic-skills training and about 5,000 workers have received remediation in the two-year colleges.[48]

As community colleges and technical schools evolve as a source of training expertise for business, in addition to changing state criteria for funding, changes are needed in the system to accredit these two-year schools.

Both individuals and employers need a community college system that provides accredited training. That is, each community college must be recognized by an accrediting body as a legitimate source of education and training. This will be particularly important as national occupational definitions and standards are adopted. Accreditation provides the quality assurance that makes individual occupational training transferable among employers, and it assures employers who contract for services from community colleges that the colleges are qualified.

The immediate problem is that current accreditation systems are designed to evaluate academic institutions and programs, not occupational programs. The accreditation systems devised for four-year academic institutions have been adapted to community colleges, and accrediting bodies have not developed the expertise to evaluate nonacademic activity.

The power accreditation bodies have over community colleges also affects the colleges' checkbooks. Federal funding for student aid, as well as other federal assistance, is based on recognition by the Accrediting Agency Evaluation Branch of the U.S. Department of Education of 6 regional accrediting associations and 12 state associations.[49] A college without recognition by one of these 18 bodies is not eligible for this federal funding. Of the six regional accreditation bodies, only two make any provision for occupational programs and institutions—the New England Association of Schools and Colleges and the Southern Association, both of which established the provisions 20 years go.[50]

There is, however, a parallel accrediting system that encompasses occupational training and is recognized by the federal government. The Department of Education recognizes over 60 specialized accrediting bodies, each of which has developed criteria for training in a specific occupation, such as engineering, law, medicine, and teaching.[51] These professional standards were established to ensure the highest possible quality in particular professions. For the most part, however, the professions involved require at least a four-year degree and therefore affect only those students in community colleges who plan to transfer to other institutions.

A more serious accreditation problem is that academic accreditation is normally based on a series of process factors—number of full-time students enrolled, quality of textbooks used, academic credentials of the teaching staff, and even the physical plant and size of library. Understandably, business people focus on results rather than process: Can the community college graduate function in the workplace as one would expect after being educated and trained?

This gap in quality assurance must be closed. An accreditation system must be devised which ensures good academic training as well as good occupational training. A number of projects are underway to close this gap, including an effort by the National Alliance of Business and the Georgia Department of Technical and Adult Education.[52] These organizations have become advocates for establishing national occupation standards and for recognition by accreditation systems of occupational curricula.

Business must press for change in the way community colleges view occupational training-education and must help them maintain their accreditation even as they become a primary source—perhaps the primary source—for workforce training.

The second problem inhibiting the shift of community colleges into a more forceful training mode is the lack of recognition by most states of the part-time, or short-time, nature of student enrollments for occupational training. This situation would change, of course, if the accreditation problem were resolved.

In the fall of 1990, the Secretary of Labor established a National Advisory Commission on Work-Based Learning to explore the feasibility of a national system of skill certification and accreditation. Business must join this effort by forming a parallel coalition that would establish a national accreditation body for occupational training. The coalition would include labor, testing organizations, and nonprofit employers, such as health providers.

At the local level, business people should become familiar with the capabilities and with the problems of community colleges, and then help them become better resources for occupational training. Business people should also identify current and projected skill needs so that these institutions can offer courses that lead to jobs. Businesses can join together to form pools of workers who need training and then contract with community colleges for it.

The community college system is clearly a potential source for developing better employees both now and in the future. Partnered with business and high schools, they can provide a smooth transition from school to work. They can also be a source of employee training and management consulting for companies too small to handle this activity internally. Business must move forcefully at the national level, at the regional and state levels, and locally to galvanize this resource.

The involvement of community colleges, high schools, and business in a skills-training partnership implies a significant change in human resource public policy in the United States. More accurately, it implies that the United States, for the first time, will have policies beyond those that have been developed to help the disadvantaged.

Federal and state governments have a broad range of possible human-resource policy issues to address. The U.S. Office of Technology Assessment has identified 16 possible roles for the federal government, including the reduction of present barriers to company training and funding training technology research.[53]

Each of these options should be studied to determine the contribution they would make to other efforts undertaken by business, but one of them should be resolved quickly. The

---

SUMMARY OF FEDERAL POLICY OPTIONS

Issue Area A: Reducing Barriers to Company Training:

1. Help firms set up training consortia
2. Expand technical assistance to trade associations and others
3. Establish limited tax credit for Corporate Training
4. Phase-in payroll-based national training levy

Issue Area B: Individual Workers and Retraining:

5. Expand apprenticeship concepts
6. Fully fund Federal vocational programs
7. Fund workplace basic skills programs
8. Provide favorable tax treatment for continuing training
9. Evaluate ways to help workers finance continuing education

Issue Area C: Training and Technology Assistance:

10. Coordinate technology and training assistance
11. Help States include training in industrial extension services
12. Support creation of an employer institute for work-based learning

Issue Area D: Improving the Effectivness and Quality of Worker Training:

13. Encourage adoption of best practice approaches and technologies
14. Fund the Federal Training Technology Transfer Program
15. Fund more civilian learning and training technology research
16. Improve the data about work-based training

Source: Office of Technology Assessment, 1990.

United States needs some sort of tax-oriented incentive system to encourage businesses to retrain their workers. This incentive would jump-start frontline worker training and enable businesses to move into high-performance work organizations much quicker than under ordinary circumstances.

Roughly, there are two approaches to tax incentives—a tax-penalty system for those who do not meet certain criteria and a tax-reward system for those who do. For example, in France, Germany, Sweden, Ireland, and Singapore, businesses either pay a payroll tax directly or pay a tax if they do not meet certain training criteria to fund government-controlled training.

In the United States, business already pays taxes used to train disadvantaged workers and to fund the various state and federal programs established to further worker training. A number of states have installed tax-oriented programs to help workers. In 1989, Mississippi became the first state to offer tax credits to companies that provide basic-skills training to workers.[54]

In those countries that utilize tax penalties as an incentive, the federal government pools these funds to pay for government-sponsored worker training. It would appear that a penalty approach would not be appropriate for the United States, because it is unlikely that the federal government would become involved in direct training of workers.

A more appropriate approach is to view frontline worker training in the same way the nation has viewed investments by business in capital equipment and in research and development (R&D). Investment tax credits have been available to business from time to time to encourage equipment purchases, and R&D tax credits have been available to encourage continuing development of the nation's technology base. In both cases, it was the country's consensus that these expenditures were vital enough to the nation's interests that business should be motivated to make them.

Surely, frontline worker training is equally important. Not only must the United States upgrade the skills of individuals to world-class standards, the business community must upgrade work organizations to improve productivity and it cannot do so without better-trained employees.

Any sort of tax relief for worker training would have to have safeguards to ensure that the right sort of training was being delivered to the right employees; managers, technical, professional, and sales personnel already receive the bulk of corporate training dollars and should not be eligible for tax relief.[55]

Although a tax credit for business would impinge on a deficit federal budget, eventually the Treasury probably would recover tax revenues through higher payroll taxes and higher corporate taxes. In addition to possible tax credits, business should press the Financial Accounting Standards Board for changes in accounting rules that would allow business to amortize frontline worker training costs rather than to expense them. Worker training is an investment in the same way that factories and equipment are investments and should be treated as such.

Business needs to make tens of billions of dollars in worker-training investments during the 1990s and then more investments to convert to high-performance work organizations. Tax and accounting treatments must be altered to make this mammoth conversion affordable.

CHAPTER 8

CLOSING THE EDUCATION GAP

Public education from kindergarten through 12th grade is one of the largest industries in the United States. It is a $225-billion-per-year business and the largest component of every state's budget.[1] Over 2 million teachers work in 83,000 public schools and in 15,000 school districts.[2] Every state, every school district, and every school has an administrative staff.

Given the size of the enterprise, there should be little surprise that it is taking years to change. It could be argued that education is adopting new forms of work organization and technology at about the same speed as the U.S. business community. To the extent that there is disagreement about new approaches to teaching, that family life affects learning ability, and that voters are reluctant to pay more taxes, the business community must exercise patience in turning this system around to the point where assessments of educational attainment and other indications of success are apparent.

But there is little question that business has a role in changing the American education system—at the federal level, the state level, and locally. In one sense, business is the customer for the product of our schools, and business should help the education system improve the quality of its output just as it would work with any vendor to upgrade performance. In wrestling with the problem of educational improvement, business people should keep in mind that there are several types of problems.

- The system attempts to sort students by ability, pushing those along who seem to have the intelligence and drive to attend college while allowing the rest to learn only enough to qualify them for low-paying jobs.

- The system is highly centralized, and teachers are not given enough freedom to deliver customized learning according to need.
- Teachers and administrators are undertrained to handle new work organizations.

Recognizing the poor performance of our education system, President Bush and our nation's governors adopted six national education goals in 1990, agreeing to work together to improve education.[3] To make the United States internationally competitive, together they pledged that by the year 2000 the following objectives would be met:

1. All children in the United States will start school ready to learn.
2. We will increase the percentage of students graduating from high school to at least 90 percent.
3. U.S. students will leave grades 4, 8, and 12 having demonstrated competency over challenging subject matter, including English, mathematics, science, history, and geography.
4. U.S. students will be first in the world in science and mathematics achievement.
5. Every adult American will be literate and possess the knowledge and skills necessary to compete in a global economy and exercise the rights and responsibilities of citizenship.
6. Every school in the United States will be free of drugs and violence and offer a disciplined environment conducive to learning.

These goals are ambitious and may not be achieved in a short time. However, they provide direction for action and guideposts against which progress can be measured. They can be the impetus for educational improvement nationwide.

The national education goals emphasize more than just scholastic outcomes for elementary and secondary school students. They also stress the importance of a student's environment, requiring improvements in children's early preparation for school and in the physical and social conditions of the schools themselves. They recognize that education is a life-long process, holding us accountable for the skills of every American adult. Furthermore, the goals are explicit about the dual purpose of education: (1) economic—preparing Americans to compete in a global economy, and (2) social—preparing Americans to "exercise the rights and responsibilities of citizenship."

Most important, though, the goals require the educational system to serve all students better, both our high achievers and our low achievers. Not only must students' skill levels improve (goals three and four), but more of our youth must stay in school and be counted among those students (goal two). The result: we cannot achieve all of the goals we have set for ourselves by catering to those students who would likely succeed even without substantial assistance. All students must be well served.

But as valuable as these goals are, they are only a first step. It is not enough just to define our goals; we must develop strategies to achieve them.

One set of strategies was announced by President Bush and the Secretary of Education in April 1991, when they proposed AMERICA 2000.[4] AMERICA 2000 represents the administration's view of how the nation can accelerate progress toward meeting the goals. To the extent that the U.S. education system has always been a state and local system—the federal government only contributes six percent of all education funding[5]—the administration has sought to exploit the niches that it and the nation's governors believe are appropriate.

AMERICA 2000 is a combination of high-exposure demonstration projects and practical advancements to the teaching art. The U.S. business community has an important role to play in the strategy, including funding and school-to-work activity.

The strategy proposed by the president has four principal elements:

1. Improve today's schools, including establishment of national standards in five core subjects and assessment systems for measuring progress.

2. Create a new generation of U.S. schools for tomorrow's students, including establishment of a new nonprofit corporation funded by business, which will award contracts for creating innovative schools.

3. Advance the notion of lifetime learning among adults who have already graduated from school, including establishment of skill standards and skill certificates for core-work proficiencies.

4. Improve conditions in communities so that students come to school prepared to learn, including communitywide programs to improve social conditions and to meet the six national goals.

These strategies and others proposed by various organizations have a common theme—they represent fundamental restructuring of the U.S. education system and the way children learn. They are not marginal programs that provide slightly better conditions, such as lengthening the school day, increasing graduation requirements, or adding a few courses targeted at the at-risk population.

However, expecting schools to improve without establishing a definition of success is like trying to win a race without knowing where the finish line is located. We must define what it is we want students to know and be able to do, we must set measurable standards for the knowledge and skills, we must develop credible instruments for assessing students against the standards, and we must then hold schools accountable for student achievement.

Of course, defining success, like establishing national education goals, is only the first step. The way schools are governed and managed must also change. If we intend to hold schools accountable for outcomes, we must give them more control over how they run the race. Many companies have discovered that they can improve productivity by moving decision making down to the factory floor. The education system should also give more control over management and curricula to schools and teachers, providing technical assistance and support from district and state offices.

Additionally, new curricula—both content and instructional strategies—must be designed to match children's various learning needs so they can meet the new standards. These curricula must enable all students to succeed in today's economic climate: to think, analyze, and solve problems, work productively in groups, and communicate effectively in both written and oral forms.

No restructuring will succeed unless the preparation and continued training of education professionals—primarily teachers—is drastically improved. Most experts feel that teachers are not adequately prepared to do the tasks expected of them today. If we add to those tasks new responsibilities for participating in school management and adapting new curricula designed to teach all students higher levels of knowledge and skills, the need for improved teacher training becomes only more apparent. The same need for training exists for administrators and other staff; their roles, too, must change dramatically.

Finally, we must recognize that the schools cannot succeed alone. Early childhood development programs are crucial if children are going to enter schools ready to learn. Continued social and health services will be necessary for many students if they are to be able to focus on their studies. Parents must be a positive force encouraging and supporting their children's development and learning at all times.

Such radical restructuring will not be easy. All sectors of society must join in a collaborative effort to bring it about. Business has a stake in ensuring that the restructuring occurs. Business also has the ability to help make it happen.

EDUCATION ASSESSMENT AND ACCOUNTABILITY: DEFINING AND RECOGNIZING SUCCESS

There are no agreed upon standards for success in American education today. Some people focus on dropout and graduation rates, others focus on Scholastic Aptitude Test (SAT) scores, and still others on student performance on other standardized tests. None of these approaches, however, assesses students against a clearly defined standard of what they should know. Because of this, improvement in composite scores at the state, district, or school level may not prove there has been an improvement in students' skills in any important area.

Additionally, many people feel that existing assessment instruments are not designed to measure the skills we most want our students to possess, such as the ability to write coherent essays, think, analyze problems, or work in groups. Most assessments today are multiple-choice, paper-and-pencil tests given at a single point in time. In contrast, the more far-sighted individuals working in the assessment field today recommend the use of such varied and multiyear assessment procedures as portfolios, exhibitions, and performance exams.

Finally, there is practically no connection between any measure of performance, albeit imperfect, and future consequences for students, teachers, schools, or school districts. Students who do poorly in school get hired for the same jobs at the same wages as those who do well.[6] Except for those who are accepted to the most elite colleges and universities, most students qualify for most schools. By and large, teachers' salaries are not dependent on any measure of their performance. And, with rare exceptions, nothing happens to the school or school district that consistently fails to provide students with a quality education.

However, things are beginning to change.

Efforts are underway across the United States to define expectations for student achievement. The National Governors' Association has formed an assessment panel to measure progress of the states in meeting the educational goals they and the president have established. The Secretary of Labor's Commission on Achieving Necessary Skills (SCANS) was created in February of 1990 as a blue-ribbon commission of business, labor, and education leaders charged with the mission of hammering out national competency guidelines that reflect work readiness.[7] Project C³, a collaborative effort involving "corporations, community, and classrooms" in Fort Worth, Texas, is also working to define workplace skills and link these back to instruction in the classrooms.[8] And in the academic arena, such organizations as the National Council of Teachers of Mathematics and the American Association for the Advancement of Science are forging consensus around the knowledge and skills students should gain in their academic disciplines.

Advances are also being made in the assessment arena. Educators in California, Connecticut, and Vermont are developing new, comprehensive assessment tools that measure student skills against specified outcome goals.

As for accountability, a number of states have implemented incentive programs that reward schools or districts for their performance on such things as test scores, pupil and/or teacher attendance, number of writing and homework assignments, enrollments in specified courses, dropout rates, and parent/community involvement. South Carolina, for example, provides financial awards for schools making the largest achievement gains compared to similar schools.[9] With bonuses for student and teacher attendance, winning schools can receive awards of up to approximately $30 per student.[10]

When districts perform poorly, South Carolina recommends a remedial action plan (with which the district must comply or face loss of funds or removal of the district superintendent) and provides technical assistance.[11] New Jersey and Kentucky laws enable the state to take over school districts that do not meet state established minimum levels of performance.[12]

The assessment and accountability movement has also made it to the national stage. Both the House and the Senate held hearings on the issue of national assessment in 1991, and numerous business and education organizations have endorsed the notion of a national assessment system.

In its most comprehensive form, a national assessment system would include (1) common definitions of what students should know and be able to do, (2) standards of performance that are established at internationally competitive levels, and (3) varied and multiyear assessments—such as portfolios, exhibitions, and performance exams—are focused on mastery of bodies of knowledge, thinking skills, and interdisciplinary problem-solving.[13]

To build this system, representatives of interested and affected groups—including academicians, politicians, educators, and local teachers, business, community organizations, and parents—should be brought together in a collaborative process to develop definitions and achievement standards. After the national standards are set, states, districts, schools, and teachers would have the flexibility to design their own curricula and instructional strategies for achieving the standards and accommodating racial, ethnic, and geographic diversity.

The Learning Research and Development Center and the National Center on Education and the Economy have organized a consortium of states and school districts willing to engage in a 10-year effort to build such a comprehensive system.

Another group, "Educate America, Inc.," is developing six 90-minute tests covering reading, writing, mathematics, American and world history, science, and geography.[14] The proposed tests (consisting of multiple-choice and performance-based items) would be administered to all students in the fall of their senior year in high school.[15]

Both proposals advocate that student performance results be used as one criteria in the selection of entrants to colleges and for employment, and as a judge of the performance of schools and districts.

The proposals are not without their critics. Concerns exist over who would define the standards, how free states and districts would be to develop their own curricula, the cost and time required to develop and administer the assessments, and whether assessment results would be used in ways that would be fair to students, schools, and districts.

If an assessment system truly is to accomplish its goal of promoting improvement in education performance, all three of the problems discussed at the beginning of this section must be addressed: (1) defining standards for success, (2) developing assessment instruments which measure students' skills against those standards, and (3) attaching consequences to student performance against the standards. If the first two problems are not resolved, the system will promote achievement of the wrong kinds of skills. If the third is not resolved, there will be no incentive to improve performance.

MANAGEMENT AND GOVERNANCE: ACHIEVING HIGH-PERFORMANCE EDUCATIONAL WORK ORGANIZATIONS

Many people believe the U.S. system of education is very bureaucratic and top-heavy with management. There are three levels of bureaucracy affecting the system—federal, state, and local. Each level has rules and regulations that must be followed by each and every public school. Former U.S. Secretary of Education William Bennett characterized the administrators who oversee these rules and regulations as "the blob," and suggested that a great deal of money could be saved if the bureaucracy was reduced.

Until 1981, federal funding of local education—between 6 and 7 percent of the national total—was primarily targeted at at-risk student populations through specific programs.[16]

In 1981, the Education Consolidation and Improvement Act[17] consolidated 29 discretionary grant programs into a block grant program entitled Chapter 2.[18] Local school systems now apply to their State Education Agency for funds rather than competing for individual program dollars at the federal level.

Critics have argued that federal rules are onerous and inflexible and that the programs themselves are too prescriptive. Advocacy groups for the specific students served by the federal funds argue for maintenance of strong federal oversight to ensure that the students continue to benefit. Over time, many states have also established specific programs for specific students.

On average, states provide 50 percent of each school's budget, with about 44 percent derived from local sources and the balance from the federal government.[19] Like the federal government, states also specify how their portion is spent. Additionally, several states set standards for materials and textbooks, frequency of testing, length of school year, plus course and graduation requirements. States also control requirements for teacher and administrator certification.

Local school districts also impose rules and regulations. Operations, management, class length, length of courses, number of class periods, staffing, and organizational matters are all mandated in many districts.

The most significant penalty paid for this large bureaucracy is not the diversion of education dollars, but the stultifying effect it has on the delivery of learning. These layers describe a top-down management system that leaves little time or ability for local innovation or customized teaching.

It doesn't have to be this way. Just as many businesses have discovered that the key to increased productivity is in pushing decision making down in the organization, so too can the education system improve the educational attainment of students by pushing decision making down to school sites.

In fact, a number of school districts have already begun this bold experiment. Districts such as Jefferson County, Kentucky; Dade County, Florida; and Rochester, New York, have caught the attention of educators and the business community with the efforts they have initiated. In most of these locations, it is too soon to judge whether or not they have been successful, but they are paving the way for a necessary change; they are helping to establish the new education paradigm.

In Manhattan's District No. 4 in East Harlem, however, schools have been allowed to operate with substantial autonomy since 1974, and the results are impressive![20] In this district, more than half of all families are headed by single females, almost 80 percent of all students qualify for free-lunch programs because of low income, and almost all students are minorities.[21] Despite these demographic conditions, 62.6 percent of the district's students were reading at or above their appropriate grade level in 1987, up from only 15.9 percent in 1973.[22] Students in this district were also dramatically more successful in gaining admission to New York's selective high schools than were students from earlier years.[23]

On a more general level, a RAND Corporation study of 13 New York City and Washington, D.C., schools, *High Schools with Character*, found that both private and public schools were significantly more effective when the schools were substantially self-managed than when the schools were bureaucratically controlled.[24] This study also focused on disadvantaged inner-city youth—by all accounts the hardest population to reach.

What does site-based management involve?

First, there must be clear goals for what the schools are expected to accomplish. If schools are to succeed, they must have commonly understood definitions of success. These goals, of course, should relate to the definitions of what students should know and be able to do as discussed in the previous section.

Second, schools must be given considerably more control over the educational process. If teachers and administrators are to be held accountable for outcomes, they should have as much control as possible over how they achieve them. What matters is whether "Johnny can read," not the process used to teach him reading. Control over the process also requires some control over the school budget. It is nearly impossible to make significant changes in instructional practices when you can't decide whether to trade textbooks for computers, teachers for counselors, or even teachers for computers!

Third, teachers, principals, and other school staff must receive training related to process, including shared decision making, risk-taking, consensus-building, conducting meetings, budgeting, as well as substance—innovations in instructional techniques. Site-based management requires school staff to take on responsibilities they have never had before, and they must be prepared to meet these challenges.

Finally, the role of the professionals at both the district and the state level will need to change significantly. Instead of promulgating regulations and monitoring school compliance, districts and states should function as consultants and advisors, offering technical assistance to schools in response to their requests. Such a major shift in mission requires more than a change in mind-set; it requires that these professionals also receive substantial training.

Site-based management is not easy to implement. Besides altering all of the roles and power relationships that currently exist in the education system, it raises a number of difficult technical issues. For example, if teachers are to join in decision making with principals, other school staff, and sometimes with parents, time must be found in teachers' days to accommodate the decision-making process. Furthermore, if teachers are to take on new roles and responsibilities, union contracts may have to be rewritten and constructed more flexibly. None of these problems are insurmountable, though, and creative schools and districts have found ways to implement site-based management despite these obstacles.

Site-based management is sometimes associated with another education-reform strategy—school choice. Defined simply, school choice is a system that enables parents to choose which school their child will attend. In some choice plans, parents can choose between sending their child to a magnet school (a school with special programs or equipment designed to attract students) or to their local neighborhood school. In others, parents can choose to send their child to any school in their district, or sometimes even to any school in the state, including private schools.

Some people believe that school choice will raise the quality of our nation's schools. They believe choice will introduce the pressures of a free-market system and that the result will be pressures for education reform. Others believe that choice will not improve the quality of education overall and will, in fact, create a two-tier market: top-quality schools for students whose parents have the interest and time to ensure their children attend the best schools and a tier of low-quality schools for all others.

If school choice is introduced after other restructuring components have been implemented, it will increase the educational opportunities for children. After schools are freed to introduce new teaching strategies, parents will have the opportunity to choose from among different learning environments from those schools that best meet the needs of their children.

Whether or not a district or state adopts school choice, site-based management must be implemented if the schools are going to improve. No one instructional approach is likely to work for all schools and all classrooms, and that is exactly what district, state, and federal management of the schools tends to promote. The communities in which schools operate vary, the skills of the teachers vary, and the needs of the students vary. Schools must be free to assess student needs and then devise a strategy for meeting those needs and ensuring that all students are educated to internationally competitive standards.

CURRICULUM AND INSTRUCTION: EDUCATING ALL OUR CHILDREN

The U.S. system of education has evolved in a manner not designed to educate all our children. Instead, it has become a sorting mechanism, promoting some children on to higher levels of education, while relegating others to shift for themselves.

Because there used to be a rough balance between educational delivery and society's educational needs, educators were not concerned with developing and adopting curricula and instructional strategies that would increase every child's chances for success. Over time, most high school systems developed three curriculum tracks: college preparatory, vocational education, and general education. Today, only those in the first track are likely to receive a good education, and there is debate about that.[25] The vocational track is likely to be technologically obsolete and deficient in the provision of basic math, science, reading, and writing needed for today's working world. The third track was never focused enough to prepare students for future education or employment, which may explain why it has the largest number of dropouts.[26]

The most damaging aspect of this approach to education is that tracking establishes expectations in the minds of students, their parents, and their teachers—often diminished expectations. Students are put into tracks at an early age, depending on test scores, a teacher's opinion, or an expression of interest by students or parents. Poorer students are not led to believe they can attend college, slowly maturing students are tracked before they can blossom, and lazy students are permitted to coast.

Those that don't demonstrate early signs of possibility are denied possibilities because the system is not aimed at them.

But today, we cannot afford to let any child fall through the cracks. All children must succeed in learning if we are to have the kind of economy, and society, that we want.

Curricula today must be based on the definition of what all children should know and be able to do, as discussed earlier in the section on assessment and accountability. Working backward from that definition, curricula should be designed to ensure that all our children possess that knowledge and those skills when they leave our education systems. They need to know much more than a collection of facts; they need to know how to learn, think, analyze, problem solve, and work productively in groups.

Instructional methodologies must recognize that different children learn in different ways, and that different methods must be employed to meet their needs. Some children may respond well to lectures, drill, and practice, while most will need more concrete, hands-on learning experiences, such as experimentation and self-directed research. Children learn much more when what they are studying is somehow related to things that they already know and understand. They also learn more when the material is shown to be relevant to their lives—both current and future.

An example from the experience of a Vermont teacher, utilizing the portfolio system of learning assessment, is instructive, both in demonstrating the power of this type of testing and in demonstrating how children assimilate learning differently.[27]

An eighth-grade algebra class was asked to prepare in writing a convincing argument that the following statistic is possible: it is estimated that 7 percent of all Americans eat at McDonald's each day; there are 250 million Americans and 9,000 McDonald's restaurants.[28] One student answered the problem in a seven-page explanation using logic, while another compiled a complex chart showing customer flows.[29]

Both students had correct answers and all the students found the question interesting and challenging. Rather than require students to work through algebraic formulas in precisely the same manner, using hypothetical situations, real situations can be created and students can be allowed to derive correct answers in a fashion that suits their way of thinking.

This sort of teaching and problemsolving cannot be effectively mandated from a remote location. While broad definitions of what children should know and be able to do should probably be established at the national level, the specific details concerning content and instructional methods should be left to the local level. Only then can we be sure that they will be responsive to both community and student needs.

One of the leading efforts in education restructuring is the Coalition of Essential Schools, which focuses heavily on curriculum and instructional reform.[30] Led by Theodore R. Sizer, the coalition works with about 200 schools to help them adapt a set of nine common principles to their own unique situations.[31] These nine principles include embracing curricula that help students learn to use their minds well and provide students with thorough mastery and achievement in a few areas, rather than with limited knowledge and understanding in a great number of areas; adopting school practices which are tailor-made to meet the needs of every group or class of students; personalizing teaching and learning to the maximum feasible extent; and having teachers function as coaches, thus provoking students to learn how to learn.[32]

The coalition also supports an interdisciplinary curriculum design, one that makes clear the connections between what is taught in math and science, English and history, or even science and history. Making any of the changes supported by the coalition is difficult, time-consuming work.[33] But those involved think that it is worth the effort, and that they can make significant gains in ensuring that all students learn.

Technology, too, can open the doors to new instructional practices. Computers can be used to augment the teaching force, allowing students to work on some skills at their own pace with the computer while teachers focus on other skills with individuals or small groups of students. Videos and educational television programs can help students visualize scientific achievements and historical events, making the learning experience much more vivid and real to them. To be effective though, technology cannot be treated solely as the acquisition of equipment with a separate function from the main instructional strategy of the school and classroom. Instead, it must be integrated with that instructional strategy—it must reinforce and strengthen the school's existing curriculum.

In Mt. Edgecumbe High School, Sitka, Alaska, the business concept of total-quality management is being applied to restructure the educational process and redesign the school's curriculum practices.[34] Students, faculty, and administration work together to develop a consensus about the purpose of the school, and curriculum and instruction are geared toward meeting that purpose. Coursework is no longer graded. Instead, students work on projects until they consider them "perfect." Coursework is interdisciplinary: a report for an entrepreneurship course may also be required as part of an English class. This innovative program is proving successful. Forty-seven percent of the students who graduated from Mt. Edgecumbe have entered college and are still there or have graduated—a significantly better rate than the national average.[35]

Whatever path is taken to improve curriculum and instruction, two key things must be remembered: (1) curriculum and instruction cannot be successful unless they are designed to meet a clearly defined instructional goal; and (2) curriculum and instruction must be adapted to meet the needs of individual communities and students. All kids can learn, but only if our education system is flexible enough to adjust to them.

PROFESSIONAL DEVELOPMENT: WHERE THE RUBBER MEETS THE ROAD

Because, ultimately, education is delivered by teachers in classrooms, no improvement in educational outcomes can occur unless teachers are highly skilled, productive professionals.

Unfortunately, this is not always the case today. Comparisons of high school students' SAT scores suggest that our brightest students are not attracted to careers in education.[36] Additionally, schools of education frequently do not adequately prepare their students for careers in teaching, failing either to give students a grounding in the subjects they will teach, or to provide them experiences so they are adequately prepared.[37] The one- or two-semester ''clinical experience''—student teaching—is too little. One weakness is that student teachers are not placed in the classrooms of the most qualified teachers, or, equally important, in the classrooms of those who are most able to transfer their knowledge to the student teachers.[38]

Ongoing teacher development is also neglected. In-service training usually consists of short sessions on topics that are either peripheral to teachers' daily activities, or worse yet, irrelevant to most of the teachers in attendance.[39] Because teachers' salaries are linked to the number of academic credits they obtain, teachers frequently take additional courses at local colleges or universities or through extension programs, but little care is taken to ensure that these courses will have any impact on the quality of their teaching.[40]

Much needs to be done if we are to (1) attract more qualified individuals to the teaching profession, (2) better prepare them to begin their careers, and (3) ensure that they are able to update their knowledge and upgrade their instructional skills over the course of their careers.

A number of suggestions have been put forward to attract brighter candidates to a career in teaching. The most obvious is to raise teacher salaries, particularly starting salaries. Since 1983, when *A Nation at Risk* was released, average teacher salaries (in constant dollars) have risen 33 percent.[41] Rochester, New York, received national news coverage when it raised average teaching salaries in the district to $40,000 (since raised to $50,000) and established a maximum career-teacher salary of $70,000![42]

While raising salaries has been a widely practiced method of attracting potential teachers to the field, many think that a more direct approach should be used if the aim is to attract brighter students to teaching. For example, students with scores in the top 10 percent of those applying to college education programs could be offered tuition deferments that could then be written off over some number of years of their actually teaching. (A similar program could be used to attract minorities or math and science majors to teaching.)

Of course, making the profession more attractive goes well beyond raising salaries or subsidizing the cost of teacher preparation. Much has been done over the last few years to improve the image and raise the public's esteem of teachers. Public-service announcements and television specials on education, as well as lengthy articles in newspapers and magazines, have suggested that teaching is an honorable and important profession. This has not only induced recent high school and college graduates to choose teaching as a career, but it has prompted a number of individuals to make teaching their second career.

However, more than words are necessary in order to actually improve the environment in which teachers work and to make teaching more of a profession. At a very basic level, teachers could be given staff and/or computer support to handle such clerical tasks as duplicating and maintaining student records. More importantly, if teaching truly is to become a profession, real opportunities for career development and career advancement must be instituted, and teachers must have more control over curriculum and instruction and decision making in the schools.

As mentioned earlier, upgrading the quality of teachers not only requires attracting brighter individuals to the profession, but it also requires improving preservice training. The Carnegie Forum on Education and the Economy, in its 1986 report *A Nation Prepared: Teachers for the 21st Century*, recommended that a bachelor's degree in the arts and sciences be made a prerequisite for the professional study of teaching and that a new professional curriculum in graduate schools of education, leading to a master in teaching degree, be developed.[43] Such a graduate program would include both coursework based on systematic knowledge of teaching and structured internships and residencies in the schools.[44] The Carnegie report also suggests that clinical schools, modeled after teaching hospitals, be established to ensure that student teaching internships be well structured and productive.[45]

More recently, John I. Goodlad, in his book *Teachers for Our Nation's Schools,* recommended that colleges and universities create for teacher education centers of pedagogy, which have the same amount of autonomy and authority now reserved for law and medical schools.[46] In order to overcome the secondary-to-peripheral status that characterizes teacher education in most universities, these centers would have their own budgets and faculty, and the authority to design their own curricula, develop their own reward structures, control teacher internships, and limit student admissions.[47]

The Holmes Group, an organization composed of the deans of schools of education, has also recommended changes in pre-service (and in-service) teacher training. In *Tomorrow's Schools,* the group recommends the creation of Professional Development Schools, which would have four functions: (1) clinical preparation of student teachers, (2) inquiry on issues important to the school's practitioners as well as to the university's re-searchers, (3) reformation of the school to serve its own student population and community, and (4) continued learning of the school's teachers and administrators.[48]

Also under development is a system of national standards for teachers, which the states and districts are free to adopt for local hiring and teacher assessment. The National Board for Pro-fessional Teaching Standards is developing the standards using nonpublic money.

The third key ingredient to raising teacher quality is continu-ing education. Teachers need to be encouraged and supported to take courses that will improve the quality of their teaching. Furthermore, schools or districts should only provide in-service training if it is of high quality and directly related to teachers' needs.

Instead of raising teachers' salaries based on the number of outside education units they accumulate, teacher compensation could be linked in some way to teacher performance. This would encourage teachers to take courses that would improve their teaching, and create pressure from teachers to restrict in-service training programs to programs that are useful. Furthermore, if teachers are truly to be treated as professionals, they need to be compensated for their time and out-of-pocket expenses associated with continuing education.

Business, which spends billions annually on training the workforce, should be an advocate of training for the education workforce.

As education is restructured in ways outlined in earlier sections of this chapter, issues of teacher preparation and continuing education take on even greater importance. If teachers are to join with school administrators and other school staff in management of the schools, they will need training in management and decision-making techniques (as do frontline workers in business settings where team production and other new work organizations are established). If they are to take a lead role in guiding curriculum and instruction in the schools, they will need to be privy to the latest innovations in challenging students' minds.

Our schools will never be better than the teachers and the managers we employ. Therefore, if education restructuring is to succeed, we must focus on the quality of our teachers and administrators.

COMMUNITY SUPPORT FOR EDUCATION

In the 19th century, responsibility for educating young people rested primarily with the family and the community; learning was an integral part of home and community life. In this century, mass immigration, industrialization, and urbanization have given impetus to a formal education system separate from the family and community.

But family and community circumstances affect the ability of children to learn. Too often, children are born premature or on drugs, receive limited health and nutritional care, or are not exposed to educational stimulation. These children are usually developmentally and educationally behind their peers before they even step foot in the schoolhouse. Those who are hungry and ill clothed, or on drugs or pregnant, frequently cannot focus on their school lessons. And those who do not receive support and encouragement from their parents are unlikely to make learning a priority.

Statistics suggest that children like these are prevalent in the United States today.

1. One in four preschoolers and one in five children live in poverty.[49] Children comprise the poorest population segment in the United States.[50]

2. The percentage of infants born to unmarried mothers reached 22% in 1985; 34% of the mothers were teens.[51] Mothers of two thirds of all preschool children will be in the workforce by 1995.[52]

3. There were an estimated 2.2 million recorded cases of child abuse or neglect in 1986.[53]

4. In 1987, 51 out of every 1,000 girls aged 15 to 19 gave birth.[54] More than 100 of every 1,000 black girls in this age group gave birth.[55]

If schools are to educate all of our children, problems such as these must be addressed. Children need to arrive at our schoolhouse doors ready to learn, they need to receive assistance in overcoming problems that might distract them from their studies, and they need to receive support from their parents throughout their school careers.

Early childhood development services may be the best investment we can make in our nation's future. Each $1 spent on nutrition supplements for poor women, infants, and children saves $3 in later health-care costs.[56] Providing childhood immunizations saves $10 in later medical costs.[57] And quality preschool education can return $5 in reduced costs for special education, public assistance, and crime for every $1 invested.[58]

The nation must develop a national policy aimed at delivering a comprehensive array of services for a child's development needs. Health-care services must include prenatal care; pediatric checkups and treatment (vision, hearing, developmental, and physical examinations and immunizations); and proper nutrition. Early educational stimulation is also critical. Through play and social interaction, children can develop language, thinking, and social skills, and a healthy curiosity for learning.

Early childhood development services such as these can be provided by individual families or the community, with private or public resources, through a single all-inclusive program, or through coordination of a number of service providers. The right delivery mechanism depends on the specific needs of children and their families, family skills and resources, and available private and public child-development programs in a community.

Once children enter school, their needs for comprehensive services do not evaporate. If schools are to be successful, they must become locations where a myriad of needed services are available to the students, either because the services are delivered at the school site, or because the services are readily accessible nearby. Schools must either be provided with the resources and training needed to carry out social and health services themselves, or they and other institutions must join together to provide the services.

Cities in Schools, Inc. has promoted programs to reposition existing community service personnel into 183 schools across the country.[59] New Jersey has funded 29 school-based centers providing mental health and family counseling, health services, substance abuse programs, and employment services at a single site.

On a broader level, the Casey Foundation has sponsored the New Futures initiative in seven cities.[60] As part of this initiative, "oversight collaboratives," representing all the key education, business, and social service groups in each city, work together to develop new policies and programs and promote fundamental improvement in the way services are delivered to young people.[61] In Portland, Oregon, the Portland Investment ties together school, employment, and social services polices and programs through a broadly representative council called the Leaders' Roundtable.[62]

While community support services are important, parental involvement in education is crucial if children are going to succeed. By the time they are 18, children will have spent only about

9 percent of their lives in school. Parents must set the stage for their children's success in learning by seeking prenatal care and maintaining healthy diets and lifestyles during pregnancy; ensuring that their children receive needed healthcare and preventive services; and serving as first teachers, helping their children to use their minds and to explore their environments. They must also stress the importance of learning, show their children that learning opportunities extend far beyond the four walls of a classroom, and help their children succeed in educational endeavors.

Not all parents are prepared to do this. Programs such as Parents as Teachers in Missouri train parents to maintain healthy and safe homes and to encourage their children's language, thinking, and social skills development.[63] The National Center for Family Literacy in Kentucky combines training in parenting with training in education and work skills because they recognize that parents can best serve their children when the parents are skilled and self-confident.[64]

Schools can serve as the conduit for programs such as these. Additionally, schools can encourage and facilitate parents' involvement in their children's education by setting convenient hours for parent-teacher conferences; sending home newsletters and bulletins about school activities; establishing parent ombudsmen to focus on answering parental concerns; and operating parent outreach programs to pursue parental involvement and to keep parents informed.

Dr. James P. Comer, professor of child psychiatry at the Yale Child Study Center, developed a program that involves parents as decision makers and volunteers in the schools, helping to bridge the gap between the home and school environments.[65] Every Chicago school has a local school council, consisting of 10 elected members—six parents, two teachers, and two community representatives—plus the school principal, with the authority to hire the principal and develop a school-improvement plan and school budget.[66] These, and programs like them, go a long way toward encouraging parental involvement in children's education.

Improving education in the United States requires a much broader effort than one focused solely on the schools themselves. Early childhood programs, integrated social and health services, and parental involvement are crucial ingredients which cannot be omitted.

BUSINESS STRATEGIES TO IMPROVE EDUCATION

If our national education goals are to be attained, all five of the issues discussed in this chapter—assessment and accountability, management and governance, curriculum and instruction, professional development, and community support—must be addressed. Not only are all five important, but they are all interconnected. Solving the problems in any one of the areas requires solving the problems in the other areas as well.

The task is enormous, far too big and important to be left to the education community alone. Our entire society has a stake in the outcome of education restructuring, and our entire society must band together to work toward its success.

Business can play a major role in ensuring that success. Business wields tremendous clout in the political arena and can be a powerful advocate for educational change and for those educators who are attempting to establish a new education paradigm. Business also has the expertise to communicate the need for change so that taxpayers and other voters endorse political leadership. Additionally, while the world of business does not directly translate to the world of education, there are many things that do translate, or could with minor modifications, and business can share its relevant expertise with education. While financial contributions from business could never, and should never, replace adequate financing of education, some corporate contributions might be used to leverage important changes or finance short-term or interim projects. Business can volunteer its employees to directly assist students, teachers, and schools; and it can establish programs and policies to facilitate and promote employee support of education.

When most policymakers or educators are asked what business can do to promote education restructuring, they immediately focus on the role business can play as a vocal and persistent advocate for change. All too often, business is asked only for financial assistance or to act in an advocacy role, but it is not asked to make substantive contributions to the education process. Business people are comfortable in an advocacy role and with providing funds, but too often uncomfortable in the role of actually becoming involved with the education change process.

But the possibilities are limitless. Business can support the creation of a national assessment system. It can support increased funding for early childhood development programs, research and demonstration projects to improve curriculum and instruction, and development of assessment and accountability systems. Business can lobby for eliminating rules and regulations at the federal, state, and district level that impede site-based management or make it difficult for localities to integrate existing social and health services to better serve the needs of children.

Business likes to focus on results—called outcomes in the education world—and not on the education process, with which it is unfamiliar. The fact is, however, that there is much about education that is similar to business, and educators can use business experience.

Decentralization, shared decision making, training, risk-taking, technology—these are concepts common to restructuring in the business community and in the education community as well.

Business-education joint ventures that explore these common traits are needed. Strategies must be developed to chart the course of change, with appropriate responsibilities assigned to business people, educators, and political leaders.

This activity can take place at the local, state, and federal levels. Business leaders must analyze their resources and determine how they can best contribute to the education-improvement effort. In some cases, this may be no more than joining an ongoing effort in a community or in a state. Existing coalitions can always use additional leverage. Some companies are in a position to join the effort at all levels and in many communities, an activity that requires a comprehensive plan and commitment.

In considering how to help, businesses should study five broad categories of activity: (1) advocacy, (2) communications, (3) expertise, (4) financial, and (5) employee involvement.

Advocacy can be as simple as a letter to senators and congressmen at the federal level, or letters to state-level representatives. The range of possibilities is broad and could include meetings with elected officials and education administrators on subjects as simplistic as a call for better schools or as complex as advocacy for a specific reform measure, such as school-based management or a comprehensive assessment system.

In trying to match available resources to possible activity, it's important that business people study the issues. Understanding education reform and the politics of education allows advocates to decide how to approach the situation and provides them with knowledge that makes their advocacy credible.

Communications includes the effort to convince parents and educators that change is needed. Sometimes, communications with the public is needed to help educators and elected officials achieve the improvements they are seeking. Business people are in a good position to testify to the inadequacy of schools. Most voters don't have children in schools,[67] and most parents who do don't believe there is anything wrong with their schools.[68]

This activity will probably issue from a collaborative of some sort, either at the state level or at the local level. These programs must be creative and convincing. It would probably be wise to enlist the assistance of advertising, or public relations agencies, and business people with experience in managing the output of this talent.

Expertise is an area that has to be custom-tailored to the improvement desired. That is, business can loan expertise to school districts and schools in order to save money (purchasing, facility maintainance and construction, computer systems, staffing), or to improve talent (teacher recruiting, training for teachers and administrators, familiarization with workplace needs, management techniques).

Both management and governance, and professional development, are areas in which business has a great deal of expertise to offer education. The movement toward decentralization and employee empowerment began in the business sector, and those who have worked through implementation themselves are in a perfect position to help districts and schools. Business can also draw on its expertise in personnel management to help districts and schools develop recruitment and retention strategies to improve the quality of teachers in the field, as well as continuing-education policies that ensure training is relevant to teachers' skill needs.

An analysis is required in cooperation with schools to determine where business experts can best help. It's vital that business and education also determine in advance what it is they expect as a result of the collaboration. If reduced costs is the goal, it should be specific as to where the savings might accrue and it should be understood that sometimes one has to make an investment to save money. The key here is to be realistic about the possibilities so that the education community as well as the business community don't exit the experience disappointed because of unrealistic expectations.

Financial assistance to schools must be approached carefully. For instance, it does little good simply to purchase a few computers for a school and to expect improvement in student performance. Computers are systems that require as much teacher training as they do student training. Appropriate computer programming must be purchased, and the computers must be integrated into the curriculum in a sensible fashion.

The best approach to direct financial assistance to schools is to use it to leverage change in some way. Thus, money should be donated to schools for computers only after the schools have prepared a written plan demonstrating how the computers would be used to improve curriculum and instruction. Money for social and health services might be provided if a school district prepares a plan showing it will integrate existing community services into the schools.

Employee participation can take many forms, depending on the commitment of the company. Employees can be exhorted to help their schools, or employees can be given time off from work to do so.

Employees have served as guest lecturers in classrooms, and as tutors or mentors for individual students. Such personal, face-to-face relationships benefit both the students and the employees. Students gain a better understanding of the world of work and feel part of the larger community. In all too many cases, their relationships with the employees may be the only link they have with responsible, caring adults. Employees, on the other hand, usually experience personal satisfaction from their interactions with the students, and they gain a more concrete understanding of the problems confronting both the students and the schools. While these personal interactions do not bring about the systemic changes needed to achieve the national education goals, they may stimulate further activities on the part of the employees and their companies.

Finally, businesses must recognize that many of their employees are also parents, and therefore their own internal programs and policies need to support employees' involvement in education. Flex-time or administrative leave might be needed to help employees juggle day care services, attend teacher conferences, or just visit their children's classrooms from time to time. If children are to start school ready to learn, employee health benefits must cover prenatal care for women and pediatric services for children.

Businesses can provide additional support to employees either by helping them to locate quality day care programs (that have educational components) or by subsidizing some of the costs. At the worksite, classes could be provided on such topics as good parenting skills, how to help a child do well in school, and how to handle your child's discipline or drug problems.

Businesses that want to make a real difference in education must internally put in place the systems and structures that will make it possible to deliver on their promises over many years. For example, businesses may wish to encourage employees to run for election to school boards and make sure that they have enough time off to fulfill their commitments if they are elected. Company and employee commitment to educational change must become part of the corporate culture. To accomplish this, company CEOs and boards of directors must make clear, personal commitments to education restructuring. In larger companies, the CEO should designate one individual, with direct access to him or her, to provide day-to-day leadership for the corporation's education efforts.

The Business Roundtable—an organization of the chief executive officers of about 200 large corporations—has formed an Education Task Force with a 10-year commitment to help restructure the education system in each of the 50 states. Partnering with the state governors, these executives are working to remove the impediments and add the incentives that will cause change at the local level.

Additionally, key executives with expertise useful to the education restructuring effort, could serve on a corporationwide council to develop the company's education strategy and coordinate various departments' efforts in education. These executives should be experts in such areas as community affairs, human resources, education and training, public relations, government relations, the corporate foundation, marketing and communications, and selected operating divisions and field locations.

While a single company could engage in some of the activities outlined above on its own, many of the more systemic changes could best be accomplished through community collaboratives comprised of representatives of a number of businesses in the area, as well as education, government, and community leaders. Such coalitions must work together to understand education issues, identify critical problems, establish goals, and develop a plan of action. As a group, coalition members can have a substantive, long-term impact on the direction of our nation's schools.

There is little debate that the education system in the United States must be improved so that U.S. business can become more competitive in the decades ahead. The business community has the resources as well as the management expertise to kick-start the recent stall in the national historic continuum of learning progress. Business people must make a contribution to this effort as they step up activities to train workers and to reorganize the workplace.

CHAPTER 9

CLOSING THE
PUBLIC–POLICY GAP

With the final collapse of the centralized, controlled economies of Eastern Europe and the U.S.S.R., it is likely that the last decade of this century will be remembered mainly as the decade that witnessed the historic triumph of the free-market system. A hallmark of that free enterprise system is a labor market in which employers and workers enjoy the freedom and flexibility to adapt to change. It is essential that we preserve that freedom to innovate and find creative solutions as we face the competitive challenges of the future.

However, just as our individual education, training, and management systems are no longer adequate to bridge the education, training, and work organization gaps that confront us, our traditionally fragmented approach to the solution of these problems no longer effectively serves the efficient operation of U.S. labor markets.

During the long era of U.S. economic preeminence when workforce performance issues were of marginal concern, individual initiatives by business, government, and other groups were also at the margin and thus could be pursued in a largely ad hoc, uncoordinated fashion. Because of advances by our international competitors and the ease with which business can operate around the globe, there must now be a sea change in both the level and range of business' commitment, at the community level, to the solution of our workforce problems and comparable efforts by the public and nonprofit sectors. The aggregation of these efforts must be a new cohesive, high-performance education and training system.

A theme common to all the challenges posed in this book is the need for business to take the lead in building, at the local level, new systems to attack the problems of an underdeveloped frontline workforce:

1. New business-education partnerships to close the education gap.
2. New school-to-work-transition systems and better work training to close the training gap.
3. New forms of decentralized work organization within their firms.

Each of these newly established systems contributes to achieving a single overarching objective that should be at the top of the priority list in each of our communities—to improve and continually upgrade the workforce of those communities. Yet, in the United States, no locus of responsibility exists for achieving that critical national goal. Thus, our current employment and education initiatives, both public and private, and those basic systemic changes we propose for the future will take place in an institutional vacuum unless a new institution is constructed.

While we are building new arrangements to solve our local education, training, and work-organization problems, we must also begin working toward the establishment of new local management systems that will link these efforts, gear them to the unique needs of individual labor markets, and integrate them with the services of other public and nonprofit training and education agencies.

To fill this management gap in our labor markets, we must establish in each of these areas, a business-led, private-public human-resources development system to serve as both catalyst for change and to provide a management structure that will ensure that change is accomplished with the most efficient use of private and public resources.

There is abundant precedent for government cooperation with the private sector beyond traditional tax incentives and loans to small businesses. This additional help has ranged from technical assistance to motivational programs. In recent years, the U.S. Department of Commerce has sponsored a program that is affecting the way businesses view their operations. The Malcolm Baldrige National Quality Awards program was initiated by Public Law 100–107 for the purpose of providing models of total-quality achievement for other U.S. companies.[1] Manufacturing companies, service companies, and small businesses are eligible for the three types of awards made annually.

The first awards were made in 1988, and the business community has already embraced them as a leading indicator of good management. In 1990, over 180,000 applications were requested from the Commerce Department and there were just three winners.[2] Many companies require their suppliers to complete the application because the extensive application process also constitutes an excellent operational review exercise.

This sort of governmental leadership and attention regarding a topic of importance to business and to the nation is an important adjunct to work-organizational efforts. Many companies have altered their approach to employee involvement as a result of installing total-quality systems. Other programs in the Department of Commerce and in the Labor Department have also helped develop and communicate best practice techniques.

The United States has a century-long policy of helping entrepreneurial farmers. Land-grant colleges have long provided the R&D for the nation's agricultural systems, and the Department of Agriculture Extension Service provides technical assistance throughout the nation to ensure the spread of best practices in this vital segment of the economy. This national policy has led to U.S. agricultural leadership.

Thus, business should not be uncomfortable or fearful about calling for governmental involvement in human-resource matters—there is little difference between a state-operated agricultural college helping farmers and a local community college helping manufacturers and other traditional businesses.

A community-based human resources development system is often called a labor-market board because the boards are normally organized to manage the affairs of specific labor markets in the United States.

Although labor markets offer the framework for organizing government resources, every community must also form suborganizations to meet their needs and to tap the labor-market boards described here—a Community Human Resource Development System.

The establishment of labor-market boards will represent more than an administrative structure. The boards will also reflect a consensus that had been reached within each community—among business, labor, the schools, training agencies, and the public at large—that the education, training, and organizational challenges we face are of central concern and that only a broad public-private partnership at the local level can successfully meet these challenges.

It is time to build such a system—a network of labor market boards that will serve every labor-market area in the United States. The nucleus of this system is already in place in over 600 cities and counties across the nation—the business-led Private Industry Councils (PICs) that administer job-training programs under the Job Training Partnership Act (JTPA). PICs operate much like the English Training and Enterprise Councils except that they are limited to overseeing programs aimed at the disadvantaged and displaced workers; they are business directed and performance oriented.

In the discussion that follows, we will outline the basic structure of a U.S. labor-market board system and then suggest how we can move from where we are to successfully put it in place using the PICs as a core.

The boards' basic objectives in their communities would be to ensure the following:

1. That education and training programs are adequately preparing participants with the basic and occupational skills required in the labor market.
2. That high standards of performance have been established for these programs and are being achieved.
3. That currently disparate services are linked and delivered as cohesive delivery systems.

4. That the totality of both private and public efforts is adequate to meet the needs of the local economy.

The scope of the boards' programmatic responsibility would be broad and inclusive. In one way or another, they should impact upon all public and private education and training for front-line workers in their communities. Only through such broad coverage can the boards be of optimum service by providing easier access to a broad array of services for youth and adults, reducing administrative costs for program managers, and providing a rational system with which employers can readily interact.

These potential areas of responsibility may be viewed in terms of three broad categories:

1. Federal and state programs for which the PICs currently have responsibility and which could be readily reassigned to their successor labor-market boards.

2. Other federal or federal-state programs for which the boards could acquire responsibility either through amendment of existing legislation or through new administrative arrangements.

3. New initiatives, such as those described in earlier chapters, in which the boards' role would be the result of negotiation with the local business and education communities.

The two principal programs that could be readily transferred to the labor market boards' jurisdiction are the local employment and training programs authorized under JTPA and the operations of the U.S. Employment Service.

Under the largest JTPA program, federal Department of Labor (DOL) grants are provided through the states to over 600 cities and counties to operate job-training programs for economically disadvantaged youth and adults in those localities. The program authorizes a full range of training and employment services and encourages coordination with other local human-service agencies.

A second JTPA program provides grants to the same localities to provide summer jobs and remedial services for school-age disadvantaged youth. The PICs presently have statutory authority for these programs in concert with locally elected officials.

The Employment Service (ES) is funded through federal (DOL) grants to the states and provides placement and related labor-exchange services through a network of 1,700 local ES offices. Under current law, local ES plans must be developed in consultation with and be approved by the PICs, with any disagreements ultimately resolved by the Secretary of Labor. While few PICs have actually asserted this authority, it could be used more actively by labor-market boards to integrate labor-exchange services into a broader local workforce development system.

A large number of federal and federal-state programs would be logical components of comprehensive local workforce development systems. Some are fully or primarily funded by the federal government. Others are funded primarily by the states with the federal government contributing a minority share. In all cases, the services are delivered locally. To acquire labor-market board responsibility for these programs would require amendment of existing legislation or negotiated administrative arrangements between the boards and the relevant state and local governments or private administering agencies.

JTPA National Programs. These programs provide training and employment services to specific target groups: Indians and native Americans; migratory and seasonal farmworkers; older workers; and severely disadvantaged youth through residential Job Corps centers. All of these programs are administered through federal contracts or grants with specific specialized organizations.

JTPA Grants. These grants to the states provide retraining services for dislocated workers. These grants are administered by substate grantees designated by the governors under agreements with the locally elected officials and PICs of those areas. However, while the grantee may be the local PIC, that is not currently mandated in the law.

Job Opportunities and Basic Skills Program (JOBS). JOBS is a comprehensive new program enacted to provide recipients of federal Aid to Families with Dependent Children (AFDC) with education and training services that will enable them to achieve self-sufficiency. It is funded through Department of Health and Human Services grants to the states and is administered locally by state or county welfare agencies. Significantly, the legislation requires that the PICs be consulted by state and local welfare agencies in selecting service providers and in identifying appropriate training and job opportunities in the area. In some states, such as Maryland, a decision has been made to administer JOBS through the JTPA system, thus placing the PICs in a key position to link the program with JTPA and other services.

Vocational Rehabilitation. This is a program of federal grants to the states to provide training, counseling, rehabilitation, and related services for handicapped individuals to enable them to become employable. It is administered locally through state and local rehabilitation agencies.

Vocational Education. Vocational education, like education generally, is funded and administered by the states and local jurisdictions. The federal Department of Education (ED) provides grants to the states and local education agencies designed to improve vocational education for specific groups, such as the disadvantaged, the disabled, and individuals with limited English proficiency, who face special barriers in the job market. While federal grants represent only about 10 percent of total vocational education funding, these funds can be used to leverage change at the local level.[3] As in the case of JOBS, the PICs already have a statutory role to play in this program. Federal vocational legislation—the Perkins Act—requires that cooperative arrangements be established between local education agencies and the PICS to avoid duplication and to increase the accessibility of vocational education services.

Adult Basic Education. This program of federal (ED) grants to the states provides support for adult literacy and basic-skills programs. It is administered through local education agencies and other organizations that provide literacy training.

Just by focusing these existing federal programs under a business-managed umbrella agency would provide an impressive array of tools to address the needs of those individuals in the local population with particularly serious education and skills deficiencies, particularly the economically disadvantaged and the long-term unemployed.

But the gaps we face pervade the entire workforce, not just the disadvantaged. Local business leadership, through the labor-market boards, will need to take the initiative to structure local solutions to the problems confronting our mainstream workforce. These boards would be the vehicle for stimulating action and orchestrating resources to carry out new initiatives. To help close the local education gap, labor-market boards would be the catalyst for the formation of business-education collaboratives in their areas. The specific role of the collaboratives would vary depending on the needs of each locality. The boards would be in a unique position to analyze those needs and help shape an appropriate response from the business community.

To help close the local training gap, labor-market boards, with representatives from education as well as business, would serve as broker between employers and the schools in negotiating the development of the new structures needed to ensure that noncollege-bound youth are prepared to make the transition from school to work. Beyond the school-to-work transition, the boards would serve as advocates in the community for the concept of lifelong learning, making the case to employers as well as to workers that a continuing investment in training is essential for their mutual economic survival; the boards could make the necessary linkages between employers, workers, and local educational institutions such as community colleges, voc-tech institutes, and private proprietary schools.

To help close the organizational gap, the boards would extend their advocacy to the way firms organize their work processes, urging employers to move toward decentralized, high-performance work organizations. Indeed, the concepts of life-long learning investment and building a high-performance work organization are integrally related and would be advocated as two dimensions of the solution to the organizational gap between U.S. business and its overseas competitors.

The length of this inventory of possible programs and initiatives that would be within the scope of responsibility of a new labor-board mechanism is somewhat arbitrary. The list could be longer or shorter. However, to the extent that a board has a wide range of tools at its disposal, it will be able to meet the needs of the local labor market more effectively.

Functionally, the boards are likely to play a different role with respect to each of the programs within their jurisdiction. They would have direct programmatic responsibility for certain functions, such as the training and retraining of disadvantaged and dislocated workers and the operation of the labor exchange services of the Employment Service.

In carrying out its responsibilities to bring about needed changes in the schools and within firms, the board would serve as advocate, communicator, and, where requested, provider of technical assistance. Crosscutting and undergirding all these functions, the boards would be the source of statistical labor-market and career information in the community. This information would also serve as the basis for devising an overall local-area workforce development plan that would set priorities, articulate performance goals, and guide the planning for each of the workforce development services provided within the community.

Under our pluralistic system, the boards must have a membership that is fully representative of the community if they are to coordinate these diverse education and training resources in each locality. However, the philosophy underlying the specific composition of the labor-market boards is the same as the original rationale for the composition of the PICs. As the primary consumers of the product of the local education and training system, private employers should chair the boards and constitute the majority of the board's membership. We should also emulate the British TECs and require that the business members be at the leadership levels of their firms. The boards should also include the principal service providers in the locality—the heads of the local education agencies, community colleges, public and private training organizations, the Employment Service—as well as representatives of labor and community organizations.

While the boards will be locally based and locally oriented, their establishment is in response to the compelling national priority we have discussed in these pages—the need to rebuild the U.S. workforce. Thus, there is a basic federal role to be played in this process. Labor-market boards would be authorized to carry out certain federal program responsibilities. However, in order to qualify and be funded, boards would have to carry out the more comprehensive role described above. Boards would also be expected to supplement federal funding with state, local, and private funds reflecting the broad scope of responsibility they negotiate with agencies and organizations in their areas.

The state role would also be crucial. Local education, training, and labor-market services are, in a large part, the responsibility of the states, in many cases under federal-state programs. A major commitment is needed by the nation's governors and state legislatures to ensure the viability of the local labor-market board concept. To gain this commitment, the boards, with the support of the federal government, need to demonstrate to the governors and the legislatures that tangible benefits will accrue to state government with the boards' establishment. They will need to make the case that, rather than simply creating another administrative layer, the boards can bring greater efficiencies to service delivery and substantially upgrade the quality of the workforce with resultant benefits to the locality and the state as a whole.

One state, Massachusetts, has already made such a commitment. Beginning in 1982, the state government called upon the PICs to take on responsibility for training and education programs in addition to JTPA. These have included state welfare training, refugee education, dropout prevention, and adult literacy programs. In 1988, legislation was enacted to broaden the PICs' role in Massachusetts. They were renamed Regional Employment Boards and given the responsibility to "oversee and provide policy guidance" for additional state-funded employment, training, and employment-related education programs. At least one other state, Connecticut, is currently moving in this direction.

The concept of a national network of labor-market boards represents a significant change in the way education and training programs are managed at the local level. It provides for a new, active presence in local communities that would be pressing for high standards of quality and efficiency in the delivery of services. Labor-market boards would be significant because of their statutory responsibility for key federal programs in a locality. They would actively negotiate for a substantive role with respect to nonfederal programs and services. While federal legislation may be desirable at some point in the future, much can be accomplished administratively under present legislation. The business community must begin now, under current legislation, to build a national system of labor-market boards and then a system for human-resource development in every U.S. community.

The logical starting point for this process is the PICs. While they have been fully operational for less than a decade, the PICs have established themselves in over 600 cities and counties as business' primary link with local, publicly supported job-training programs. The PICs were established in the final years of the Comprehensive Employment and Training Act (CETA) under the 1978 reauthorization legislation, and were charged with administering a small-scale, private sector-oriented training program.

In writing CETA's successor legislation, JTPA, Congress and the administration recognized that if the new legislation was to be truly successful in training and placing workers in private-sector jobs, only the local business community could ensure that success. The PICs were given substantive responsibility, along with local elected officials, for JTPA's mainline local training programs for economically disadvantaged youth and adults and for the summer youth employment program. The legislation became fully operational in 1983.

In the intervening years, JTPA has compiled a record of success in training and placing disadvantaged persons in private-sector jobs—a record without precedent in the 30-year history of federal employment and training programs. The program's ties with business and industry, through the PICs, were, in large part, responsible for that success. As a result, during this period, Congress has steadily broadened the PICs' role to include advisory and other responsibilities for non–JTPA programs such as the Employment Service, vocational education, and welfare training.

The task of rebuilding the U.S. workforce will require the full commitment of U.S. business, the federal government, and the states. Creating an institutional structure at the local level to spearhead that effort will take no less a commitment.

As in the case of AMERICA 2000, the president's education reform program, the responsibility for rebuilding our workforce must be lodged at the local level. However, as a challenge of urgent national importance, there is a leadership responsibility at the national and state levels. A national coalition of the administration, the nation's governors, and U.S. business can create the impetus that will facilitate the process of establishing labor-market boards in each of our communities. National and state leadership efforts can be reinforced through a highly visible program of demonstration projects in which model labor-market board arrangements are developed in a series of representative localities.

This national leadership coalition could be supported by teams made up of business, federal, and state government experts that can work with PICs and their communities to begin the process of establishing local boards.

Business can accelerate formation of labor-market boards by working with the PIC system and by communicating with congressional representatives. It is time to organize education and training systems in every community in the United States.

As the federal government builds consensus in the nation to address the importance of preparing frontline workers for more productive and rewarding careers, it should also establish a symbol of this importance. The U.S. Department of Labor should establish a recognition program that honors employers who invest in their workforces. Businesses should desire this recognition every bit as much as they now desire the Malcolm Baldrige National Quality Award. In the case of workforce recognition, however, the award should not be competitive, but should be awarded to every business that meets certain criteria for worker training.

A similar system was established in the United Kingdom in 1990. Called *Investors in People*, the award goes to companies that demonstrate that they believe employees are an investment, not a cost. The program is administered through local Training and Enterprise Councils, Britain's version of local labor-market boards similar to the boards outlined above. Thus, although the program has been established centrally, with national standards for accomplishment, local organizations are empowered to review applications and to make awards.[4]

The national standards for an Investors in People award are as follows:

1. Makes a public commitment from the top to develop all employees to achieve its business objectives.[5]
2. Regularly reviews the training and development of its people.
3. Takes action to train and develop individuals on recruitment and throughout their employment.
4. Evaluates the investment in training and development to assess achievement and improve future effectiveness.

This brief summary of the national standards is backed by a lengthy explanation of the intent of each of the four points.

This innovative national program grew from the investigations of a National Training Task Force established to upgrade the quality of Britain's workforce. In 1988, the task force published its report—Employment for the 1990s—which recommended formation of the Training and Enterprise Councils (TEC), which are now being established throughout the country. The task force also recommended the Investors in People program as a method of heightening business awareness of the need to focus on human resources. The program document includes some familiar language:

> Today, many U.K. companies find themselves uncomfortably positioned between two groups of competitors: the low-cost producers from newly emerging economies, and competitors from advanced nations that are either more cost-efficient, or offering more sophisticated, high value-added products or services.[6]
>
> Ultimately, the only source of continuous improvement is people. The way that one company organizes, manages, motivates, develops, and makes use of the individual skills of its people determines whether it is more or less productive and efficient than a comparable competitor. Whilst this is widely acknowledged by companies, it is not always acted upon—often because they do not know how.

Like many of its Western European neighbors, the U.K. government has adopted as a national economic policy the development of its people and has put into place a mechanism for helping business do just that—Training and Enterprise Councils and a national recognition program for employers who meet national standards.

It is past time for the U.S. government to take a leadership role in ensuring the development of its people. Labor-market boards and other activity outlined here, including recognition for companies that ensure their employees realize their potential, should be established as quickly as possible.

Rebuilding America's Workforce:
A Business Strategy for Action and Advocacy

ACTION

Within the firm:

- Reevaluate the organization of work and introduce new high-performance work organization.
- Modernize and expand internal training policies.

Within the community:

- With school systems, establish business/education collaboratives.
- Serve on Private Industry Council and build toward labor-market board.
- Establish links with local community colleges.

At the state level:

- Through business representatives on state job training, vocational education, and other councils, help establish policies to encourage coordinated, demand-oriented programming at the local level.

At the national level:

- Through trade associations, participate actively in formulation of new workplace training policies in the administration and the Congress to assure that they are responsive to the new realities of the national and international marketplace.

ADVOCACY

Within the community:

- Promote the restructuring of schools to ensure higher levels of performance for all students and the responsiveness of curricula to occupational requirements.
- Work toward building a community consensus on human investment goals to parallel and support action on establishing labor-market boards.

At the state level:

- Advocate adequate funding of school restructuring.
- Press for legislative action to remove barriers to local coordination of training, education, and economic development policies.

At the national level:

- Participate in national campaign to promote labor-market boards.
- Promote legislation to provide for training-tax credits.
- Encourage adoption of national system of occupational certification being developed by Workplace Learning Commission.

Labor-Market Boards' Roles and Functions

Functions*

Program	Provide Labor Market Information	Review/ Incorporate Individual Plans into Area-wide Plans	Develop/ Oversee Integrated Employment Training Delivery System	Direct Program Responsibility	Promote, Assist with, Training and Technical Assistance
JTPA youth, adult training	●	●	●	●	
Other JTPA programs	●	●	●		
Employee Service	●	●	●	●	
JOBS welfare training	●	●	●		
Vocational education	●	●	●		
Adult basic education	●	●	●		
Private proprietary schools	●	●			
Community colleges	●	●			
Economic development agencies	●	●			
Business-Education collaborations	●	●			●
Firms' internal work organization & training	●				●

*The boards will, in large part, negotiate their scope of functional responsibility locally. The functional distribution presented here represents an optimum arrangement; the actual range of functions will vary from one board to another.

CONCLUSION

It's fairly easy to observe economic trends and then to project them in a way to predict the future. A great many of the nation's potential problems described in this book are based on just that sort of analysis. It's also true that a busy national leadership can become preoccupied with the near term and leave the future to its successors. If the trends are unheeded and the leadership is short-term-oriented, or Pollyannish, the trends will indeed come to fruition.

Our industrial competitor nations have observed these same trends and gauged the will of Americans. They have concluded that the United States is already over the hill and will be the third ranking economic power during this decade, behind a unified Europe and Japan. To reverse this decline and to prove our competitors wrong, U.S. leadership—business and political—must adopt a long-term view. Education and training systems must be upgraded so that our businesses are receiving top-notch workers as soon as possible. A nationwide system of public-private councils must be established to build an integrated human resource development system at the local level. Business must reorganize the workplace to achieve greater productivity.

But business must upgrade its current workforce even as it helps establish a new U.S. workforce preparation system for future workers. Business leaders competing internationally need help now with worker training and workplace reorganization. Business people who are struggling to improve profits need help now in providing remedial education and training to their workforces.

Fortunately, much of the infrastructure needed for these new systems is already in place. It is fragmented and many obstacles impede its use, but business is in a position to move swiftly to organize and to exploit existing systems. Local educators in high schools and community colleges can help business even as they build new and improved institutions.

The foundation of this activity, however, is an attitude in the United States that must be formed, or reshaped. Americans must soon arrive at a consensus that all of our citizens, not just our college trained, must receive world-class preparation for work and citizenship, which is the only way we can achieve a high-skill, high-wage economy. Parents must motivate their children to pursue value-added careers that don't require four-year college degrees. Americans must stop worrying about exporting low-paying jobs and start insisting that businesses upgrade work and create high-paying jobs.

To undertake the broad range of activity required to reverse today's economic trends will require nothing less than a national mandate. The nation's education system must be radically restructured; most of the nation's workplaces must be reorganized; nearly all current workers must be retrained, and some must even be made literate; a nationwide web of human resource development organizations must be established.

But business will not be able to galvanize public opinion regarding worker development until the business community itself decides that worker training is the most productive investment it can make. Worker training must receive first call on scarce dollars traditionally reserved for research and development and plant expansion. If U.S. business does not believe this, none of the other measures discussed in this book will be taken. There is no point to improving the education of workers if their abilities are not unleashed, if their skills are not continuously upgraded, and if their efforts are not rewarded by good jobs paying good wages.

Hopefully, we have helped convince business people that they must become missionaries for saving the United States from becoming a second-class nation. Although it has seemed otherwise for a very long time, the truth of the matter is there is no manifest destiny for the United States to insure that it will remain the leading economic power on the globe. America's economic future is in the hands of its business people.

APPENDIX

Sources

1. American Productivity & Quality Center—Founded in 1977, the Productivity Center is a nonprofit membership organization that conducts original research, publishes brochures and books, and conducts seminars related to productivity improvement. The Center focuses on techniques to improve productivity through better utilization of people, rather than technology. An extensive information center available to the public is maintained on productivity and quality subjects.

American Productivity and Quality Center
123 Post Oak Lane
Houston, Texas
77024
713-681-4020

2. The American Society for Training and Development— This is a professional association for people involved with training in corporations and as consultants. Although the society's advocacy for increased training of frontline workers may appear to be self-serving, its studies and reasoning are valuable contributions to the discussion of workforce quality. ASTD publishes books, reports, and surveys that are useful in describing the status of worker training in the United States. The society is also a good source of information regarding worker training in other countries.

American Society for Training and Development
1630 Duke Street, Box 1443
Alexandria, Virginia 22313
703-683-8100

3. The Business Roundtable—The Business Roundtable is a member organization of large corporations dedicated to research that helps shape public policy and opinion on matters related to business interests. The Roundtable operates through a series of task forces, one of which is the Education Task Force. The Education Task Force has established a program calling for the governors of each state and the chief executive officers of Roundtable member companies to cooperate in removing the impediments and adding the incentives that will encourage education restructuring in school districts.

The Business Roundtable
200 Park Avenue
Suite 2222
New York, N.Y.
10166
212-682-6370

4. Committee for Economic Development (CED)—CED is a nonprofit organization dedicated to identifying the nation's economic problems and then proposing solutions to these problems. It attempts to build a national consensus for its proposals working through its membership of business and university leaders. CED was founded in 1942.

Committee for Economic Development
1700 K Street NW
Suite 700
Washington, D.C. 20006
202-296-5860

5. Council on Competitiveness—The Council on Competitiveness is a nonprofit organization composed of chief executive officers from business, labor, and education. It was founded in 1986 and is dedicated to improving the ability of American companies to compete in international markets. The Council has a three-part agenda: to increase public awareness of the nation's economic problems; to mobilize political will required to pursue winning economic strategies; to help develop specific public and private initiatives. The Council conducts original research on business and economic matters and publishes its findings.

Council on Competitiveness
900 17th Street NW
Suite 1050
Washington, D.C. 20006
202-785-3990

6. The National Alliance of Business—This is a business-backed nonprofit organization that focuses on workforce issues. It works with the nation's Private Industry Councils in their efforts to retrain disadvantaged and displaced workers. The Center for Excellence in Education helps businesses form partnerships aimed at restructuring the K–12 system. Its workplace learning section assists businesses with school-to-work programs, workplace literacy problems, and other employee issues. NAB also advocates policy and other changes in Washington and builds consensus through a nationwide information program.

National Alliance of Business
1201 New York Ave. NW
Washington, D.C. 20005
202-289-2888

7. National Center on Education and the Economy—This organization published *The Report of the Commission on the Skills of the American Workforce* in June 1990. The study pinpoints the choice America has regarding its future—"High Skills or Low Wages." It traces the decline in wages and productivity in the United States and compares U.S. attitudes and systems to those in other nations. The Commission makes five recommendations for addressing the problems of workforce quality, including business incentives and public-sector organizations. The study was based on interviews with 550 companies and officials located in six countries, plus standard statistical comparisons. The Commission was cochaired by Bill Brock, Ira Magaziner, and Ray Marshall.

National Center on Education and the Economy
1341 G Street, NW
Suite 1020
Washington, D.C. 20005
202-783-3668

8. The National Commission for Employment Policy—This organization is an independent agency of the federal government that analyzes employment and training issues and then recommends policy to the president and the Congress. The commission was originally established in 1973 and has been reauthorized several times since. Its budget is fixed by law and its volunteer commissioners are appointed by the president. The commission sponsors original research and holds public hearings and then publishes its findings and recommendations.

National Commission for Employment Policy
1522 K Street NW
Suite 300
Washington, D.C. 20005
202-724-1545

9. National Governors Association (NGA)—NGA is the organization through which the nation's governors influence the development and implementation of national policy. The association has seven committees: Economic Development and Technological Innovation; Energy and Environment; Human Resources; International Trade and Foreign Relations; Justice and Public Safety; and Transportation, Commerce, and Communications. The Association conducts policy research and publishes educational materials regarding a range of topics.

National Governors Association
444 North Capitol Street
Suite 250
Washington, D.C. 20001
202-624-5300

10. The Office of Technology Assessment of the U.S. Congress—In addition to ongoing studies, in September 1990, OTA published *Worker Training: Competing in the New International Economy*. This comprehensive report covers the status of the U.S. workforce, training approaches in the United States and in other nations, and a number of federal policy options regarding worker training. It reports statistics, case histories, and current workplace practices. It is probably the most detailed study of this subject that has been published. The OTA project staff was headed by Lionel S. Johns.

Report
Superintendent of Documents
Government Printing Office
Washington, D.C. 20402-9325
GPO # 052-003-01214-6 ($12.00)

11. U.S. Department of Commerce—Department of Commerce funds original research on business matters and administers a range of other business support programs. The Department's Clearinghouse for State and Local Initiatives on Productivity, Technology, and Innovation provides a central repository of information regarding state and local programs aimed at stimulating economic development, including programs for training workers. The Commerce Department also administers the Malcolm Baldrige National Quality Awards program, an annual competition to identify companies operating best practices in the area of quality production of goods and services.

U.S. Department of Commerce
Herbert Hoover Building
14th & Constitution Ave., NW
Washington, D.C. 20230
202-377-2000

12. The United States Department of Labor (DOL)—DOL has published and sponsored a number of studies and commissions related to worker training and workforce preparedness.

- *Investing in People: A Strategy to Address America's Workforce Quality*—September 1989—is a study by the Secretary of Labor's Commission on Workforce Quality and Labor Market Efficiency. A panel of business, education, and labor officials published this first study of the American workforce problem and called for action by the public and private sectors.
- The Secretary's Commission on Achieving Necessary Skills was established in late 1989 for the purpose of defining workplace skills that schools should develop in students as they are taught basic academic subjects.
- National Advisory Commission on Work-Based Learning was established in 1990 to advise the Secretary of Labor on

ways to increase the skill levels of American workers, including adoption of a voluntary system for accreditation and skills certification.

U.S. Department of Labor
200 Constitution Ave. NW
Washington, D.C. 20210
202-523-6666

13. Work in America Institute—Founded in 1975, the Institute conducts research on workplace subjects aimed at improving productivity and employee effectiveness. Research findings are published and discussed at membership forums. The organization, which includes business people as well as labor leaders, also acts as a network for members interested in new forms of work organization. It has formed two managers' networks: The Work in America Managers Network for High Commitment Systems is for managers of high-performance work organizations already in place. The New Futures Network is for members who are transforming existing sites into high-performance organizations.

Work in America Institute
700 White Plains Road
Scarsdale, N.Y.
10583
914-472-9600

NOTES

Introduction

1. Sylvia Nasar, "American Revival in Manufacturing Seen in U.S. Report," *New York Times*, February 5, 1991, p. D8.

2. J. J. Servan-Schreiber, *The American Challenge* (New York: Atheneum, 1968), p. 29.

3. National Center on Education and the Economy, *America's Choice: High Skills or Low Wages!* The Report of the Commission on the Skills of the American Workforce, June 1990, p. 3.

4. C. Jackson Grayson and Carla O'Dell, *American Business: A Two-Minute Warning* (New York: The Free Press, 1988), p. 8.

5. Archie E. Lapointe, Nancy A. Mead, and Gary W. Phillips, *A World of Differences: An International Assessment of Mathematics and Science* (Princeton, N.J.: Educational Testing Service, 1989), p. 13.

6. Grayson and O'Dell, *American Business: A Two-Minute Warning*, pp. 8–9.

7. U.S. Department of Labor, Employment, and Training Administration, The American Society for Training and Development, by Anthony Patrick Carnevale, *America and the New Economy*, 1991, p. 26.

8. U.S. Department of Education, *Digest of Education Statistics: 1990*, NCES 91–660, February 1991, p. 9.

9. Ibid., p. 10.

10. Phi Delta Kappa International, *News Conference Memo*, August 14, 1990.

11. National Center on Education and the Economy, *America's Choice: High Skills or Low Wages!* p. 25.

12. Ibid., p. 9.

13. Ibid., p. 19.

14. Grayson and O'Dell, *American Business; A Two-Minute Warning*, p. 20.

15. National Assessment of Educational Progress, *Earning and Learning: the Academic Achievement of High School Juniors with Jobs*, Educational Testing Service, 1989, p. 16.

16. *The Forgotten Half: Non-College Youth in America*, Youth and America's Future, The William T. Grant Foundation Commission on Work, Family, and Citizenship, January 1988.

17. Council on Competitiveness, "Competitiveness Index," July 1991, p. 4.

18. Ibid., p. 5.

19. Paul Krugman, *The Age of Diminished Expectations: Economic Policy in the 1990s* (Cambridge, Mass.: MIT Press, 1990).

20. National Center on Education and the Economy, *America's Choice: High Skills or Low Wages!* June 1990.

21. Ibid., p. 3.

22. U.S. Department of Education, *America 2000: An Education Strategy*, 1991, p. 29.

23. Ibid.

24. American Society for Training and Development, *Training America: Strategies for the Nation*, p. 21.

25. National Center on Education and the Economy, *America's Choice: High Skills or Low Wages!* June 1990.

PART I THE COMPETITIVE GAP

Chapter 1 Overview

1. Robert B. Reich, *The Work of Nations: Preparing Ourselves for 21st Century Capitalism* (New York: Alfred A. Knopf, 1991), p. 114.

2. Ibid., p. 93.

3. Ibid.

4. Ibid.

5. Adam Smith, *An Inquiry into the Nature and Causes of the Wealth of Nations*, 1776.

6. "Consumer Electronics Survey," *The Economist* (April 13, 1991), p. 17.

7. Ibid.

8. Ibid.

9. "Those Perfidious Japanese," *The Economist* (April 20, 1991), p. 65.

10. Michael E. Porter, The Competitive Advantage of Nations (New York: The Free Press, 1990), pp. 507–8.

11. Ibid., p. 520.

12. Ibid., p. 280.

13. C. Jackson Grayson and Carla O'Dell, *American Business: A Two-Minute Warning* (New York: The Free Press, 1988), pp. 8–9.

14. Ibid., p. 9.

15. U.S. Department of Commerce, Patent and Trademark Office, *Annual Report: Fiscal Year 1989*, p. 20.

16. Reich, *The Work of Nations: Preparing Ourselves for 21st Century Capitalism*, p. 146.

17. John Akers, "Let's Get to Work on Education," *The Wall Street Journal* (March 20, 1991).

18. Ibid.

19. Grayson and O'Dell, *American Business: A Two-Minute Warning*, p. 85.

20. Robert Z. Lawrence, *Can America Compete?* (Washington, D.C.: Brookings Institution), 1984.

21. Grayson and O'Dell, *American Business: A Two-Minute Warning*, p. 36.

22. Ibid., p. 34.

23. National Center on Education and the Economy, the Report of the Commission on the Skills of the American Workforce, *America's Choice: High Skills or Low Wages!* June 1990, p. 19.

24. Audrey Freedman, *Productivity Needs of the United States: A Report from the Conference Board* (Washington, D.C.: The Conference Board, 1989), p. 2.

25. National Center on Education and the Economy, *America's Choice: High Skills or Low Wages!* p. 49.

26. Ibid., p. 27.

27. Reich, *The Work of Nations: Preparing Ourselves for 21st Century Capitalism,* pp. 175–79.

28. Ibid., p. 6.

29. Ibid., p. 104.

30. Congress of the United States, Office of Technology Assessment, *Worker Training: Competing in the New International Economy,* September 1990, p. 104.

31. National Center on Education and the Economy, *America's Choice: High Skills or Low Wages!*

32. Educational Testing Service, Policy Information Center, *From School to Work,* 1990, p. 2.

Chapter 2 The Work Organization Gap

1. Congress of the United States, Office of Technology Assessment, *Worker Training: Competing in the New International Economy,* September 1990, p.114.

2. Ibid.

3. Ibid.

4. Ibid.

5. Ibid., p. 110.

6. Ibid.

7. Ibid.

8. Ronald Henkoff, "Make Your Office More Productive," *Fortune* (February 25, 1991), pp. 72, 76.

9. Towers Perrin and The Hudson Institute, *Workplace 2000: Competing in a Seller's Market. Is Corporate America Prepared?* July 1990.

10. Congress of the United States, *Worker Training: Competing in the New International Economy,* p. 101.

11. Ibid., p. 102.

12. National Center on Education and the Economy, the Report of the Commission on the Skills of the American Workforce, *America's Choice: High Skills or Low Wages!* June 1990, p. 32.

13. Ibid.

14. John Greenwald, "Workers: Risks and Rewards," *Time*, April 15, 1990, p. 43.

15. National Center on Education and the Economy, *America's Choice: High Skills or Low Wages!* June 1990, pp. 39, 40.

16. C. Jackson Grayson and Carla O'Dell, *American Business: A Two-Minute Warning* (New York: The Free Press, 1968), p. 8.

17. Bureau of Labor Statistics press release.

18. Henkoff, "Make Your Office More Productive," pp. 78, 82.

19. Ibid.

20. Ibid.

21. Ibid.

22. Ibid.

23. Ibid.

24. Ibid.

25. Bruce Beier and Mary Gearhart, "Productivity vs. Profit Sharing," *Automotive Industries*, April 1990, pp. 53–56.

26. "Today's Leaders Look to Tomorrow," *Fortune*, March 26, 1990, p. 30.

27. U.S. Department of Education, *America 2000: An Education Strategy*, 1991, p. 29.

28. John F. Krafcik, "Triumph of the Lean Production System," *Sloan Management Review* (Fall 1988), pp. 41–52.

29. Ibid.

30. Ibid.

31. Congress of the United States, *Worker Training: Competing in the New International Economy*, p. 105.

32. U.S. General Accounting Office, *Foreign Investment: Growing Japanese Presence in the U.S. Auto Industry*, GAO/NSIAD 88-111 (Washington, D.C.), p. 52

33. Ibid.

34. William B. Scott, "Aerospace/Defense Firms See Preliminary Results from Application of TQM Concepts," *Aviation Week and Space Technology*, January 8, 1990, pp. 61–63.

35. Dun & Bradstreet Comments on the Economy (April/May 1990), p. 2.

36. Frank Swoboda, "Union Leader, Managers Pull Strings in 'Team' Programs," *The Washington Post*, April 14, 1991, p. H2.

Chapter 3 The Training Gap

1. Federal Minister of Education and Science, Germany, *Report on Vocational Education and Training: 1989*, Part I, p. 4.

2. *The Forgotten Half: Pathways to Success for America's Youth and America's Future*, The William T. Grant Foundation Commission on Work, Family, and Citizenship, November 1988, p. 4.

3. American Society for Training and Development, National Center on Education and the Economy: *Training America: Strategies for the Nation*, by Anthony P. Carnevale and Janet Johnston, 1989, p. 18.

4. Congress of the United States, Office of Technology Assessment, *Worker Training: Competing in the New International Economy*, September 1990, p. 91.

5. Ibid.

6. Ibid.

7. Ibid.

8. Ibid.

9. Ibid.

10. Ibid.

11. Ibid.

12. Ibid.

13. Ibid.

14. Ibid.

15. Ibid., p. 233.

16. Ibid.

17. Ibid.

18. Educational Testing Service, Policy Information Center, *From School to Work*, 1990, p. 5.

19. William B. Johnston and Arnold H. Packer, *Workforce 2000: Work and Workers for the 21st Century*, Indianapolis, June 1987.

20. George Silvestri and John Lukasiewicz, "Projections of Occupational Employment, 1988–2000," *Monthly Labor Review*, 112 (November 1989), p. 62.

21. Ibid.

22. Congress of the United States, *Worker Training: Competing in the New International Economy*, p. 97.

23. Ibid., p. 156.

24. Ibid.

25. Ibid.

26. Beverly Geber, "Industry Report 1990: Budgets Barely Budge," *Training*, October 1990, p. 42.

27. John F. Krafcik, "Training and the Auto Industry: International Comparisons," a report prepared for the Office of Technology Assessment under contract N3–1910, February 1990.

28. Ibid.

29. Congress of the United States, *Worker Training: Competing in the New International Economy*, p. 15.

30. American Society for Training and Development, *Training America: Strategies for the Nation*, p. 46.

31. Ibid.

32. Ibid.

33. "More Executives Go Back to School," *Fortune*, March 25, 1991, p. 12.

34. Ibid.

35. Ibid.

36. American Society for Training and Development, *Training America: Strategy for the Nation*, p. 228.

37. Congress of the United States, *Worker Training: Competing in the New International Economy*, p. 228.

38. Ibid.

39. *The Wall Street Journal*, November 3, 1988.

40. Ibid.

41. Ibid.

42. Ibid.

43. Ibid.

44. Ibid.

45. Ibid.

46. "Companies Teaching Workers 3 Rs to Compete in Age of High Technology," *New York Times*, May 1, 1988, Section 1, p. 26.

47. Congress of the United States, *Worker Training: Competing in the New International Economy*, p. 112.

48. Ibid., pp. 167–68.

49. American Society for Training and Development, *Training America: Strategies for the Nation*, p. 27.

50. Ibid.

51. Ibid.

52. Ibid.

53. Ibid.

54. Ibid.

55. Ibid.

56. Ibid.

57. Ibid.

58. Ibid.

59. Burt S. Barnow, Amy B. Chasanov, and Abhay Pande, *Financial Incentives for Employer-Provided Worker Training: A Review of Relevant Experience in the U.S. and Abroad,* Urban Institute Policy Memorandum under U.S. Department of Labor contract #99-9-0421-75-081-01, March 19, 1990, p. 43.

60. Ibid., pp. 43–44.

61. Ibid., p. 42.

62. Ibid., p. 49.

63. Ibid., p. 10.

64. American Society for Training and Development, *Training America: Strategies for the Nation,* p. 23.

65. Barnow, Chasanov, and Pande, *Financial Incentives for Employer-Provided Worker Training: A Review of Relevant Experience in the U.S. and Abroad,* p. 46.

66. Ibid., p. 33.

67. Ibid., p. 34.

68. Ibid.

69. Ibid.

70. Ibid., p. 35.

71. American Society for Training and Development, *Training America: Strategies for the Nation,* pp. 29, 30.

72. Ibid.

73. United States General Accounting Office, *Training Strategies: Preparing Noncollege Youth for Employment in the U.S. and Foreign Countries,* May 1990, p. 17.

74. Ibid., p. 18.

75. Barnow, Chasanov, and Pande, *Financial Incentives for Employer-Provided Worker Training: A Review of Relevant Experience in the U.S. and Abroad,* p. 36.

76. Ibid.

77. Ibid., p. 38.

78. Ibid., p. 45.

79. Ibid.

80. Ibid.

81. Ibid.

82. Ibid.

83. "Employment for the 1990's," white paper issued by British Employment Department, Her Majesty's Stationery Office, London, December, 1988, pp. 40–43.

84. American Society for Training and Development, *Training America: Strategies for the Nation*, p. 28.

85. Ibid.

86. Ibid.

87. Ibid., p. 29.

88. Barnow, Chasanov, and Pande, *Financial Incentives for Employer-Provided Worker Training: A Review of Relevant Experience in the U.S. and Abroad*, p. 39.

89. American Society for Training and Development, *Training America: Strategies for the Nation*, p. 29.

90. Barnow, Chasanov, and Pande, *Financial Incentives for Employer-Provided Worker Training: A Review of Relevant Experience in the U.S. and Abroad*, p. 40.

91. Ibid.

92. Ibid.

Chapter 4 The Education Gap

1. C. Jackson Grayson and Carla O'Dell, *American Business: A Two-Minute Warning* (New York: The Free Press, 1988), p. 8.

2. Ibid., p. 93.

3. Ibid., p. 92.

4. Ibid.

5. Ibid.

6. Ibid., pp. 85–86.

7. Ibid., p. 88.

8. Leonard Lund and Patrick E. McGuire, *Literacy in the Work Force*, Report Number 947, The Conference Board, 1990, p. 7.

9. Ibid., p.10.

10. Ibid.

11. Ibid., p. 9.

12. Ibid.

13. National Alliance of Business, *Atlanta 2000—Its Changing Job Market and the Employment Readiness of its Workforce*, 1987.

14. Richard A. Mendel, *Meeting the Economic Challenge of the 1990s: Workforce Literacy in the South*, a report for the Sunbelt Institute (Chapel Hill, N.C.: MDC, Inc.), September 1988, p. 15.

15. National Center on Education and Economy, Report of the Commission on the Skills of the American Workforce, *America's Choice: High Skills or Low Wages!* June 1990, p. 27.

16. Timothy Egan, ''Oregon Literacy Test Shows Many Lag in Basics,'' *New York Times*, April 24, 1991, p. A23.

17. Ibid.

18. Ibid.

19. Ibid.

20. William Wiggenhorn, ''Motorola U.: When Training Becomes an Education,'' *Harvard Business Review*, July–August 1990, pp. 71–72.

21. Irwin S. Kirsch and Ann Jungeblut, *Literacy: Profiles of America's Big Adults*, National Assessment of Educational Progress, (Princeton, N.J.: Educational Testing Service, 1986), p. 3.

22. Ross. W. Winterowd, *The Culture and Politics of Literacy* (New York: Oxford University Press, 1989), p. 86.

23. William Kolberg, President, National Alliance of Business, interview KCAL (Channel 9, Los Angeles, Calif.), October 30, 1990.

24. Wiggenhorn, ''Motorola U.: When Training Becomes an Education,'' pp. 71–72.

25. Congress of the United States, Office of Technology Assessment, *Worker Training: Competing in the New International Economy*, September 1990, p. 92.

26. U.S. Department of Labor, Commission on Workforce Quality and Labor Market Efficiency, *Investing in People: A Strategy to Address America's Workforce Crisis*, A Report to the Secretary of Labor and the American People, 1989, p. 7.

27. Educational Testing Service, Policy Information Center, *The Education Reform Decade*, 1990, p. 5.

28. Dale Parnell, *The Neglected Majority* (Washington, D.C.: The Community College Press, 1985), p. 75.

29. Ibid.

30. Ibid.

31. Ibid.

32. U.S. Department of Education, National Center for Education Statistics, *Digest of Education Statistics: 1990*, NCES 91–660, February 1991, p. 10.

33. Ibid.

34. Educational Testing Service, *The Education Reform Decade*, p. 5.

35. U.S. Department of Education, National Center for Education Statistics, *Education Partnerships in Public Elementary and Secondary Schools*, by Sheila Heaviside and Elizabeth Farris, February, 1989, p. 2.

36. Educational Testing Service, *The Education Reform Decade*, p. 12.

37. Ibid.

38. Ibid.

39. Ibid.

40. Ibid., p. 17.

41. Ibid., p. 16.

42. Ibid., p. 18.

43. Ibid., p. 17.

44. Ibid., p. 15.

45. Ibid.

46. Ibid., p. 18.

47. Ibid.

48. Ibid., p. 24.

49. National Center on Education and the Economy, *America's Choice: High Skills or Low Wages!* p. 27.

50. U.S. Department of Education, *Digest of Education Statistics: 1990*, NCES 91–660, February 1991, p. 10.

51. Ibid.

52. *An America That Works: The Life-Cycle Approach to a Competitive Work Force*, a statement by the Research and Policy Committee of the Committee for Economic Development, Library of Congress Cataloging-in-Publications data, 1990.

53. *Children in Need: Investment Strategies for the Educationally Disadvantaged*, 1987.

54. William J. Baumol; Sue Anne Batey; and Edward N. Wolff, *Productivity and American Leadership: The Long View* (Cambridge, Mass.: MIT Press, 1989).

55. Ibid., p. 197.

56. Congress of the United States, *Worker Training: Competing in the New International Economy*, p. 79.

57. Ibid.

58. Richard Kazis, "Education and Training in the United States: Developing the Human Resources We Need for Technological Advance and Competitiveness," Working Paper of the MIT Commission on Industrial Productivity, 2 (Cambridge, Mass.: MIT Press, 1989), p. 25.

59. William B. Johnston and Arnold H. Packer, *Workforce 2000: Work and Workers for the 21st Century* (Indianapolis, Ind.: The Hudson Institute, June 1987), p. 97.

60. U.S. Department of Education, *Digest of Education Statistics: 1990*, p. 25.

61. Phi Delta Kappa International, News Conference Memo, August 14, 1990.

62. The Gallup Organization for Times Mirror, January-February 1989.

63. John Immerwahr, Jean Johnson, and Adam Dernan-Schloss, *Cross Talk: The Public, the Experts, and Competitiveness*, a research report from the Business-Higher Education Forum of the Public Agenda Foundation, February 1991, p. 11.

64. Ibid.

PART II CLOSING THE COMPETITIVE GAP

Chapter 5 Overview

1. National Center on Education and the Economy, *America's Choice: High Skills or Low Wages!* The Report of the Commission on the Skills of the American Workforce, June 1990, p. 3.

2. U.S. Department of Education, National Center for Education Statistics, *Digest of Education Statistics: 1990*, NCES 91–660, February 1991, p. 10.

3. Thomas S. Kuhn, *The Structure of Scientific Revolution* (Chicago: University of Chicago Press, 1962).

4. Archie Lapointe, Nancy A. Mead, and Gary W. Phillips, *A World of Differences: An International Assessment of Mathematics and Science* (Princeton, N.J.: Educational Testing Service, 1989), p. 13.

5. U.S. Department of Education, *Digest of Education Statistics: 1990*, p. 10.

6. Congress of the United States, Office of Technology Assessment, *Worker Training: Competing in the New International Economy*, p. 84–85.

7. Ibid.

8. Ibid.

9. Ibid.

10. Ibid.

11. Ibid.

12. Ibid.

13. Ibid.

14. Ibid.

15. Ibid.

16. Ibid.

17. Ibid.

18. Ibid.

19. Ibid.

20. Ibid.

21. Burt S. Barnow, Amy B. Chasanov, and Abhay Pande, *Financial Incentives for Employer-Provided Worker Training: A Review of Relevant Experience in the U.S. and Abroad*, Urban Institute Policy Memorandum under U.S. Department of Labor contract #99-9-0421-75-081-01, March 19, 1990, p. 43.

22. National Commission for Employment Policy, *Older Workers: Prospects, Problems, and Policies*, 9th Annual Report, 1985, p. 3.

23. Barnow, Chasanov, and Pande, *Financial Incentives*, pp. 42–43.

Chapter 6 Closing the Work Organization Gap

1. U.S. Department of Education, National Center for Education Statistics, *Digest of Education Statistics: 1990*, NCES 91–660, February 1991, p. 108.

2. C. Jackson Grayson and Carla O'Dell, *American Business: A Two-Minute Warning* (New York: Free Press, 1988), p. 8.

3. Congress of the United States, Office of Technology Assessment, *Worker Training: Competing in the New International Economy*, September 1990, p. 91.

4. Thomas C. Hayes, "Behind Wal-Mart's Surge, a Web of Suppliers," *New York Times*, July 1, 1991, p. D1.

5. Congress of the United States, Office of Technology Assessment, *Worker Training: Competing in the New International Economy*, p. 115.

6. Ronald Henkoff, "Make Your Office More Productive," *Fortune* (February 25, 1991), p. 76.

7. Ibid.

8. Ibid.

9. Ibid., pp. 78, 82.

10. Ibid.

11. Ibid.

12. Ibid.

13. Ibid.

14. Ibid.

15. Ibid.

16. "Quality Is Becoming Job One in the Office, Too," *Business Week*, April 29, 1991, p. 52.

17. Ibid.

18. Ibid.

19. Ibid.

20. Ibid.

21. Ibid.

22. John Greenwald, "Workers: Risks and Rewards," *Time*, April 15, 1991, p. 42.

23. Ibid.

24. Malcolm Baldrige National Quality Awards: 1990 Award Winner.

Chapter 7 Closing the Training Gap

1. Congress of the United States, Office of Technology Assessment, *Worker Training: Competing in the New International Economy*, September 1990, p. 11.

2. *The Forgotten Half: Non-College Youth in America*, Youth and America's Future, The William T. Grant Foundation Commission on Work, Family, and Citizenship, January 1988, p. 1.

3. Congress of the United States, *Worker Training: Competing in the New International Economy*, p. 78.

4. Ibid.

5. *The Forgotten Half: Non-College Youth in America*, p. 1.

6. Congress of the United States, *Worker Training: Competing in the New International Economy*, p. 11.

7. Ibid., p. 79.

8. Ibid.

9. Ibid.

10. Jack Gordon, "Where the Training Goes," *Training*, October 1990, pp. 51–60.

11. Ibid.

12. Ibid., p. 59.

13. National Center on Education and the Economy, *America's Choice: High Skills or Low Wages!* The Report of the Commission on the Skills of the American Workforce, June 1990, p. 27.

14. Educational Testing Service, *The Education Reform Decade*, Policy Information Report, 1990, p. 18.

15. Seymour Lusterman and Leonard Lund, *Innovation and Change in Voc-Tech Education*, The Conference Board, Report Number 964, 1991, p. 17.

16. Congress of the United States, *Worker Training: Competing in The New International Economy*, p. 233.

17. Gary Moore, "Accrediting Occupational Educational Education: A New Course for the Nineties," National Alliance of Business Working Paper, March 1991, p. 16.

18. *The Forgotten Half: Non-College Youth in America*, p. 46.

19. Congress of the United States, *Worker Training: Competing in The New International Economy*, p. 55.

20. Ibid., p. 19.

21. Ibid., p. 237.

22. Ibid.

23. Ibid.

24. Ibid.

25. Ibid., p. 21.

26. Moore, "Accrediting Occupational Educational Education: A New Course for the Nineties," p. 16.

27. Ibid.

28. Ibid.

29. Congress of the United States, *Worker Training: Competing in The New International Economy*, p. 142.

30. Ibid.

31. National Center on Education and the Economy, *America's Choice: High Skills or Low Wages!* p. 78.

32. Congress of the United States, *Worker Training: Competing in The New International Economy*, p. 32.

33. Dale Parnell, *Every Student a Winner: The Case for TPAD*, 1991, p. 17.

34. *Community College Fact Book* (New York: MacMillan, 1988), p. 7.

35. U.S. Department of Education, National Center for Education Statistics, *Digest of Education Statistics: 1990*, NCES 91–660, 1991, p. 193.

36. Educational Testing Service, *The Education Reform Decade*.

37. Ibid.

38. Moore, "Accrediting Occupational Educational Education: A New Course for the Nineties."

39. Congress of the United States, *Worker Training: Competing in The New International Economy*, p. 144.

40. Ibid.

41. Ibid., p. 147.

42. Ibid.

43. Ibid., p. 148.

44. Ibid., p. 143.

45. Ibid.

46. Ibid.

47. Ibid., p. 172.

48. Ibid.

49. Moore, "Accrediting Occupational Educational Education: A New Course for the Nineties," p. 7.

50. Ibid.

51. Ibid.

52. Ibid.

53. Congress of the United States, *Worker Training: Competing in The New International Economy*, p. 28.

54. Ibid., p. 173.

55. Gordon, "Where the Training Goes," pp. 51–60.

Chapter 8 Closing the Education Gap

1. U.S. Department of Education, National Center for Education Statistics, *Digest of Education Statistics: 1990*, February 1991, pp. 27–29, 30–33, 35, 87, 154, 155, 324–26.

2. Ibid.

3. National Education Goals adopted by the members of the National Governors Association and President Bush on February 25, 1990, unpublished text.

4. *America 2000: An Education Strategy*, statement by President George Bush, April 18, 1991.

5. U.S. Department of Education, National Center for Education Statistics, *Digest of Education Statistics: 1990*, February 1991, pp. 27–29, 324–26.

6. American Society for Training and Development, National Center on Education and the Economy: *Training America: Strategies for the Nation*, 1989.

7. *The Secretary's Commission on Achieving Necessary Skills*, an unpublished text.

8. Don R. Roberts, "Fort Worth; Project C³," *Texas School Bulletin*, October 1990, p. 4.

9. Terry Peterson, Executive Director, Business-Education Subcommittee of the Education Improvement Act and Target 2000, interview, March 9, 1989.

10. Ibid.

11. Ibid.

12. Ibid.

13. National Alliance of Business Policy Statement on National Assessment, Washington, D.C., published July 12, 1991.

14. Descriptive Statement issued by Educate America, Inc., Spring 1991.

15. Ibid.

16. U.S. Department of Education, *Digest of Education Statistics: 1990*, February 1991, pp. 30–33.

17. Education Consolidation and Improvement Act, 1981, Subtitle D. Title V, Sections 551–96 of P.L. 97–35, April 13, 1981, as amended by Hawkins-Stafford Amendments of 1988 of P.L. 100–297, April 28, 1988.

18. Ibid.

19. U.S. Department of Education, *Digest of Education Statistics: 1990*, February 1991, pp. 30–33, 324–26.

20. John E. Chubb and Terry M. Moe, *Politics, Markets, and America's Schools* (Washington, D.C.: The Brookings Institution, 1990), pp. 212–14.

21. Ibid.

22. Ibid.

23. Ibid.

24. Paul T. Hill, Gail E. Foster, and Tamar Gendler, *High Schools with Character* (Santa Monica, Calif.: The RAND Corporation, 1990).

25. American Society for Training and Development, *Training America: Strategies for the Nation*, 1989.

26. Ibid.

27. Karen De Witt, "Vermont Gauges Learning by What's in Portfolio," *New York Times* (April 24, 1991), p. A23.

28. Ibid.

29. Ibid.

30. Coalition for Essential Schools, "The Common Principles of the Coalition for Essential Schools," Brown University.

31. Ibid.

32. Ibid.

33. Ibid.

34. Myron Tribus, "The Application of Total Quality Management Principles in Education at Mt. Edgecumbe High School, Sitka, Alaska," a conference paper presented in November 1990.

35. Ibid.

36. Carnegie Forum on Education and the Economy, *A Nation Prepared: Teachers for the 21st Century*, the Report of the Task Force on Teaching as a Profession, May 1986.

37. Ibid., p. 71.

38. Ibid.

39. Ibid.

40. Ibid.

41. National Education Association, *Estimates of School Statistics, 1989–90*, p. 16.

42. Rochester School District, unpublished data.

43. Carnegie Forum on Education and the Economy, *A Nation Prepared: Teachers for the 21st Century*.

44. Ibid.

45. Ibid.

46. John I. Goodlad, *Teachers for Our Nation's Schools* (Jossey-Bass Publishers, 1990).

47. Ibid.

48. The Holmes Group, *Forum*, 5, no. 2 (Winter 1990), pp. 1–2.

49. *A Children's Defense Budget: An Analysis of Our Nation's Investment in Children, FY 1989*, Children's Defense Fund, 1988, p. 282.

50. Ibid., p. xxxvi.

51. Ibid.

52. Ibid., p. 48.

53. Ibid., p. 51.

54. Ibid., p. 165.

55. Ibid.

56. *A Children's Defense Budget: An Analysis of Our Nation's Investment in Children, FY 1989*, p. 282.

57. Ibid.

58. Ibid.

59. Sarah DeCamp, Vice President for Public Affairs, Cities in Schools, Inc., interview, April 1991.

60. The Annie E. Casey Foundation's New Futures Initiative: Strategic Planning Guide, prepared by the Center for the Study of Social Policy, Washington, D.C., July 1987, pp. i–iv.

61. Ibid.

62. National Alliance of Business, *The Fourth R: Workforce Readiness*, November 1987, pp. 36–37.

63. "Involving Parents in Children's Education," *The Business Roundtable Participation Guide: A Primer for Business on Education*, April 1991, p. 73.

64. Ibid.

65. The Young and Rubicam Foundation, *The One Place: A New Role for America's Schools* (New York: St. Martin's Press, 1991), pp. 11–12.

66. "Chicago School Reform: Prodding a Lumbering Bureaucracy," *Illinois Issues*, August/September 1990, p. 37.

67. U.S. Department of Education, National Center for Education Statistics, *Digest of Education Statistics: 1990*, NCES 91–660, 1991.

68. Phi Delta Kappa International, *News Conference Memo*, August 14, 1990.

Chapter 9 Closing the Public-Policy Gap

1. The Malcolm Baldrige National Quality Awards, Malcolm Baldrige National Quality Awards: 1991 Application Guidelines.

2. Ron Zemke, "Bashing the Baldrige," *Training*, February 1991, p. 30.

3. Louis A. Ferman et al., eds., "New Developments in Worker Training," The Industrial Relations Research Association, 1990, p. 233.

4. Joseph Fischer, "PICs, REBs, and All That," National Alliance of Business, unpublished paper, September 8, 1989, pp. 2–3.

5. Ibid.

6. Ibid.

REFERENCES

Introduction

1. American Society for Training and Development. National Center on Education and the Economy. *Training America: Strategies for the Nation*. By Anthony P. Carnevale and Janet Johnston, 1989.
2. Educational Testing Service. National Assessment of Educational Progress. *Earning and Learning: the Academic Achievement of High School Juniors with Jobs*, 1989.
3. *The Forgotten Half; Non-College Youth in America*. Youth and America's Future. The William I. Grant Foundation Commission on Work, Family, and Citizenship, January 1988.
4. Grayson, C. Jackson, and Carla O'Dell. *American Business: A Two-Minute Warning*. New York: The Free Press, 1968.
5. Krugman, Paul. *The Age of Diminished Expectations: Economic Policy in the 1990s*. Cambridge, Mass.: MIT Press, 1990.
6. Lapointe, Archie E.; Nancy A. Mead; and Gary W. Phillips. *A World of Differences: An International Assessment of Mathematics and Science*. Princeton, N.J.: Educational Testing Service, 1989.
7. Nasar, Sylvia. "American Revival in Manufacturing Seen in U.S. Report." *New York Times*, February 5, 1991.
8. National Assessment of Educational Progress, *Earning and Learning: The Academic Achievement of High School Juniors with Jobs*. Educational Testing Service, 1989.
9. National Center on Education and the Economy. The Report of the Commission on the Skills of the American Workforce. *America's Choice: High Skills or Low Wages!* June 1990.
10. Phi Delta Kappa International. *News Conference Memo*, August 14, 1990.
11. Servan-Schreiver, J.J. *The American Challenge*. New York: Atheneum, 1968.
12. U.S. Department of Education. *America 2000: An Education Strategy*, 1991.

13. U.S. Department of Education. National Center for Education Statistics. *Digest of Education Statistics: 1990.* NCES 91-660, February 1991.
14. U.S. Department of Labor, Employment, and Training Administration. The American Society for Training and Development. *America and the New Economy.* By Anthony Patrick Carnevale, 1991.

Part I
The Competitive Gap: Overview

1. Akers, John F. "Let's Get to Work on Education." *The Wall Street Journal,* March 20, 1991.
2. Congress of the United States. Office of Technology Assessment. *Worker Training: Competing in the New International Economy,* 1990.
3. "Consumer Electronics Survey." *The Economist,* April 13, 1991.
4. Educational Testing Service. Policy Information Center. *From School to Work,* 1990.
5. Freedman, Audrey. *Productivity Needs of the United States: A Report from the Conference Board.* Washington, D.C.: The Conference Board, Inc., 1989.
6. Grayson, C. Jackson, and Carla O'Dell. *American Business: A Two-Minute Warning.* New York: The Free Press, 1968.
7. Lawrence, Robert Z. *Can America Compete?* Washington, D.C.: The Brookings Institution, 1984.
8. National Center on Education and the Economy. The Report of the Commission on the Skills of the American Workforce. *America's Choice: High Skills or Low Wages!* June 1990.
9. Porter, Michael E. *The Competitive Advantage of Nations.* New York: The Free Press, 1990.
10. Reich, Robert B. *The Work of Nations: Preparing Ourselves for 21st Century Capitalism.* New York: Alfred A. Knopf, 1991.
11. Smith, Adam. *An Inquiry into the Nature and Causes of the Wealth of Nations,* 1776.
12. "Those Perfidious Japanese." *The Economist,* April 20, 1991.
13. U.S. Department of Commerce/Patent and Trademark Office. *Annual Report: Fiscal Year 1989,* 1989.
14. U.S. Department of Labor. Bureau of Labor Statistics. *Occupational Outlook Quarterly,* Summer 1990.

The Work-Organization Gap

1. Beier, Bruce, and Mary Gearhart. "Productivity vs. Profit Sharing." *Automotive Industries,* April 1990.

2. Bureau of Labor Statistics press release.
3. Congress of the United States. Office of Technology Assessment. *Worker Training: Competing in the New International Economy*, 1990.
4. Dun & Bradstreet Comments on the Economy, April/May 1990.
5. Grayson, C. Jackson, and Carla O'Dell. *American Business: A Two-Minute Warning*. New York: The Free Press, 1968.
6. Greenwald, John. "Workers: Risks and Rewards." *Time*, April 15, 1991.
7. Henkoff, Ronald. "Make Your Office More Productive." *Fortune*, February 25, 1991.
8. Krafcik, John F. "Triumph of the Lean Production System." *Sloan Management Review*, Fall 1988.
9. National Center on Education and the Economy. The Report of the Commission on the Skills of the American Workforce. *America's Choice: High Skills or Low Wages!* June 1990.
10. Perrin, Towers. *Workplace 2000: Competing in a Seller's Market. Is Corporate America Prepared?* The Hudson Institute, July 1990.
11. Scott, William B. "Aerospace/Defense Firms See Preliminary Results from Application of TQM Concepts." *Aviation Week and Space Technology*, January 8, 1990.
12. Swoboda, Frank. "Union Leader, Managers Pull Strings in 'Team' Programs." *The Washington Post*, April 14, 1991.
13. "Today's Leaders Look to Tomorrow," *Fortune*, March 26, 1990.
14. U.S. Department of Education. *America 2000: An Education Strategy*, 1991.
15. U.S. General Accounting Office. *Foreign Investment: Growing Japanese Presence in the U.S. Auto Industry*. GAO/NSIAD-88-111. Washington, D.C., March 1988.

The Training Gap

1. American Society for Training and Development. National Center on Education and the Economy. *Training America: Strategies for the Nation*. By Anthony P. Carnevale and Janet Johnston, 1989.
2. Barnow, Burt S.; Amy B. Chasanov; and Abhay Pande. *Financial Incentives for Employer-Provided Worker Training: A Review of Relevant Experience in the U.S. and Abroad*. Urban Institute Policy Memorandum under U.S. Department of Labor contract #99-9-0421-75-081-01, March 19, 1990.
3. "Companies Teaching Workers 3 Rs to Compete in Age of High Technology." *New York Times*, May 1, 1988.
4. Congress of the United States. Office of Technology Assessment. *Worker Training: Competing in the New International Economy*, 1990.

5. Educational Testing Service. Policy Information Center. *From School to Work*, 1990.
6. Federal Minister of Education and Science, Germany. *Report on Vocational Education and Training: 1989*. Part I.
7. *The Forgotten Half: Pathways to Success for America's Youth and Young Families*. Final Report: Youth and America's Future. The William T. Grant Foundation Commission on Work, Family, and Citizenship, January 1988.
8. Geber, Beverly. "Industry Report 1990: Budgets Barely Budge." *Training*, October 1990.
9. Johnston, William B., and Arnold H. Packer. *Workforce 2000: Work and Workers for the 21st Century*. Indianapolis, Ind.: The Hudson Institute, June 1987.
10. Krafcik, John F. "Training and the Auto Industry: International Comparisons." A report prepared for the Office of Technology Assessment under contract N3-1910, February 1990. *Management Review*, Fall 1988.
11. "More Executives Go Back to School." *Fortune*, March 25, 1991.
12. Silvestri, George, and John Lukasiewicz. "Projections of Occupational Employment, 1988–2000." *Monthly Labor Review*. 112 (November 1989).
13. *The Wall Street Journal*, November 3, 1988.

The Education Gap

1. *An America That Works: The Life-Cycle Approach to a Competitive Work Force*. A statement by the Research and Policy Committee of the Committee for Economic Development. Library of Congress Cataloging-in-Publications Data, 1990.
2. Baumol, William J.; Sue Anne Batey; and Edward N. Wolff. *Productivity and American Leadership: The Long View*. Cambridge, Mass.: The MIT Press, 1989.
3. *Children in Need: Investment Strategies for the Educationally Disadvantaged*, 1987.
4. Congress of the United States. Office of Technology Assessment. *Worker Training: Competing in the New International Economy*, September 1990.
5. Educational Testing Service. Policy Information Center. *The Education Reform Decade*, 1990.
6. Egan, Timothy. "Oregon Literacy Test Shows Many Lag in Basics." *New York Times*, April 24, 1991.
7. The Gallup Organization for *Times Mirror*, January–February 1989.

8. Grayson, C. Jackson, and Carla O'Dell. *American Business: A Two-Minute Warning*. New York: The Free Press, 1968.

9. Immerwahr, John; Jean Johnson; and Adam Dernan-Schloss. *Cross Talk: The Public, the Experts, and Competitiveness*. A research report from the Business-Higher Education Forum of the Public Agenda Foundation, February 1991.

10. Johnston, William B., and Arnold H. Packer. *Workforce 2000: Work and Workers for the 21st Century*. Indianapolis, Ind.: The Hudson Institute, June 1987.

11. Kazis, Richard. "Education and Training in the United States: Developing the Human Resources We Need for Technological Advance and Competitiveness." Working Paper of the MIT Commission on Industrial Productivity, 2, Cambridge, Mass.:The MIT Press, 1989.

12. Kirsch, Irwin S.; and Ann Jungeblut. *Literacy: Profiles of America's Big Adults*. National Assessment of Educational Progress. Princeton, N.J.: Educational Testing Service, 1986.

13. Kolberg, William. President. National Alliance of Business. Interview. KCAL (Channel 9, Los Angeles, Calif.), October 30, 1990.

14. Lund, Leonard, and Patrick E. McGuire. *Literacy in the Work Force*. Report Number 947. Washington, D.C.: The Conference Board, Inc., 1990.

15. Mendel, Richard A. Meeting the Economic Challenge of the 1990s: Workforce Literacy in the South. A Report for the Sunbelt Institute. Chapel Hill, N.C.: MDC, Inc., September 1988.

16. National Alliance of Business. *Atlanta 2000—Its Changing Job Market and the Employment Readiness of Its Workforce*, 1987.

17. National Center on Education and the Economy. The Report of the Commission on the Skills of the American Workforce. *America's Choice: High Skills or Low Wages!* June 1990.

18. Parnell, Dale. *The Neglected Majority*. Washington, D.C.: The Community College Press, 1985.

19. Phi Delta Kappa International. *News Conference Memo, August 14, 1990*.

20. U.S. Department of Education. National Center for Education Statistics. *Digest of Education Statistics: 1990*. NCES 91-660, February 1991.

21. U.S. Department of Education. National Center for Education Statistics. *Education Partnerships in Public Elementary and Secondary Schools*. By Sheila Heaviside and Elizabeth Farris, February, 1989.

22. U.S. Department of Labor. Commission on Workforce Quality and Labor Market Efficiency. *Investing in People: A Strategy to Address America's Workforce Crisis*. A Report to the Secretary of Labor and the American People, 1989.

23. Wiggenhorn, William. "Motorola U.: When Training Becomes an Education." *Harvard Business Review*, July–August 1990.

24. Winterowd, W. Ross. *The Culture and Politics of Literacy*. New York: Oxford University Press, 1989.

Part II
Closing the Competitive Gap: Overview

1. Barnow, Burt S.; Amy B. Chasanov; and Abhay Pande. *Financial Incentives for Employer-Provided Worker Training: A Review of Relevant Experience in the U.S. and Abroad*. Urban Institute Policy Memorandum under U.S. Department of Labor Contract 99-9-0421-75-081-01, March 19, 1990.

2. Congress of the United States. Office of Technology Assessment. *Worker Training: Competing in the New International Economy*, 1990.

3. Kuhn, Thomas S. *The Structure of Scientific Revolutions*. University of Chicago Press, 1962.

4. Lapointe, Archie E.; Nancy A. Mead; and Gary W. Phillips. *A World of Differences: An International Assessment of Mathematics and Science*. Princeton, N.J.: Educational Testing Service, 1989.

5. National Center on Education and the Economy. The Report of the Commission on the Skills of the American Workforce. *America's Choice: High Skills or Low Wages!* June 1990.

6. National Commission for Employment Policy. *Older Workers: Prospects, Problems, and Policies*. 9th Annual Report, 1985.

7. U.S. Department of Education. National Center for Education Statistics. *Digest of Education Statistics: 1990*. NCES 91-660, February 1991.

Closing the Organization Gap

1. Congress of the United States. Office of Technology Assessment. *Worker Training: Competing in the New International Economy*, 1990.

2. Grayson, C. Jackson, and Carla O'Dell. *American Business: A Two-Minute Warning*. New York: The Free Press, 1968.

3. Greenwald, John. "Workers: Risks and Rewards." *Time*, April 15, 1991.

4. Hayes, Thomas C. "Behind Wal-Mart's Surge, a Web of Suppliers." *New York Times*, July 1, 1991.

5. Henkoff, Ronald. "Make Your Office More Productive." *Fortune*, February 25, 1991.

6. *Malcolm Baldrige National Quality Awards: 1990 Award Winner*.

7. "Quality Is Becoming Job One in the Office, Too." *Business Week*, April 29, 1991.
8. U.S. Department of Education. National Center for Education Statistics. *Digest of Education Statistics*, 1990.

Closing the Training Gap

1. *Community College Fact Book*. New York: Macmillan, 1988.
2. Congress of the United States. Office of Technology Assessment. *Worker Training: Competing in the New International Economy*, September 1990.
3. Educational Testing Service. *The Education Reform Decade*. Policy Information Report, 1990.
4. *The Forgotten Half: Non-College Youth in America*, Youth and America's Future: The William T. Grant Foundation Commission on Work, Family, and Citizenship, January 1988.
5. Gordon, Jack. "Where the Training Goes." *Training*, October 1990.
6. Lusterman, Seymour, and Leonard Lund. *Innovation and Change in Voc-Tech Education*. The Conference Board, Report Number 964, 1991.
7. "Manufacturing: Less Is More." *The Economist*, May 25, 1991.
8. Moore, Gary. "Accrediting Occupational Educational Education: A New Course for the Nineties." National Alliance of Business Working Paper, March 1991.
9. National Center on Education and the Economy. The Report of the Commission of the Skills of the American Workforce. *America's Choice: High Skills or Low Wages!* June 1990.
10. Parnell, Dale. *Every Student a Winner: The Case for TPAD*, 1991.
11. U.S. Department of Education. National Center for Education Statistics. Office of Educational Research and Improvement. *Digest of Education Statistics*. NCES 91-660, 1991.

Closing the Education Gap

1. *America 2000: An Education Strategy*. Statement by President George Bush, April 18, 1991.
2. The Annie E. Casey Foundation's New Futures Initiative: Strategic Planning Guide. Prepared by the Center for the Study of Social Policy. Washington, D.C., July 1987.
3. Carnegie Forum on Education and the Economy. *A Nation Prepared: Teachers for the 21st Century*. The Report of the Task Force on Teaching as a Profession, May 1986.
4. "Chicago School Reform: Prodding a Lumbering Bureaucracy." *Illinois Issues*, August/September 1990.

5. *A Children's Defense Budget: An Analysis of Our Nation's Investment in Children.* Children's Defense Fund, FY 1989.
6. Chubb, John E., and Terry M. Moe. *Politics, Markets, and America's Schools.* Washington, D.C.: The Brookings Institution, 1990.
7. Coalition for Essential Schools. "The Common Principles of the Coalition for Essential Schools." Brown University.
8. DeCamp, Sarah. Vice President for Public Affairs. Cities in Schools, Inc. Interview, April 1991.
9. Descriptive Statement issued by Educate America, Inc., Spring 1991.
10. De Witt, Karen. "Vermont Gauges Learning by What's in Portfolio." *New York Times*, April 24, 1991.
11. Education Consolidation and Improvement Act, 1981. Subtitle D. Title V. Sections 551-596 of P.L. 97-35, April 13, 1981. As amended by Hawkins-Stafford Amendments of 1988 of P.L. 100-297, April 28, 1988.
12. Goodlad, John I. *Teachers for Our Nation's Schools.* Jossey-Ball Publishers, 1990.
13. Hill, Paul T.; Gail E. Foster; and Tamar Gendler. *High Schools with Character.* Santa Monica, Calif.: The RAND Corporation, 1990.
14. The Holmes Group. *Forum.* 5. no. 2, Winter 1990.
15. "Involving Parents in Children's Education." *The Business Roundtable Participation Guide: A Primer for Business on Education,* April 1991.
16. National Alliances of Business. *The Fourth R: Workforce Readiness,* November 1987.
17. National Education Association. *Estimates of School Statistics, 1989-90.*
18. National Education Goals adopted by the members of the National Governors Association and President Bush on February 25, 1990. Unpublished text.
19. Peterson, Terry. Executive Director. Business-Education Subcommittee of the Education Improvement Act and Target 2000. Interview, March 9, 1989.
20. Phi Delta Kappa International. *News Conference Memo,* August 14, 1990.
21. Roberts Don R. "Fort Worth: Project C^3." *Texas School Bulletin,* October, 1990.
22. Rochester School District. Unpublished data.
23. *The Secretary's Commission on Achieving Necessary Skill.* An unpublished text.
24. Tribus, Myron. "The Application of Quality Management Principles in Education at Mt. Edgecumbe High School, Sitka, Alaska," November 1990.

25. The Young and Rubicam Foundation. *The One Place: A New Role for America's Schools*. New York: St. Martin's Press, 1991.
26. U.S. Department of Education. National Center for Education Statistics. *Digest of Education Statistics*, February 1990.

Closing the Public-Policy Gap

1. *Investors in People: An Initial Briefing Pack for TECs and LECs*. Briefing Documents #1–3, October 1990.
2. Ferman, Louis A., et al., eds. "New Developments in Worker Training." The Industrial Relations Research Association, 1990.
3. Fischer. "PICs, REBs, and All That." National Alliance of Business. Unpublished paper, September 8, 1989.
4. The Malcolm Baldrige National Quality Awards. *Malcolm Baldrige National Quality Awards: 1991 Application Guidelines*.
5. Zemke, Ron. "Bashing the Baldrige." *Training*, February 1991.

INDEX